Praise for Norman Solomon's Work

It is impossible to read *The Habits of Highly Deceptive Media* and not have your perceptions—of what media, news, information, and culture really are—challenged and transformed.

—Jill Nelson
author, *Volunteer Slavery* and *Straight, No Chaser*

The bold, muckraking tone of these columns offers a welcome respite from the decerebrated discourse that too often passes for contemporary journalism.

—*Los Angeles Times*

Some of the best press-bashing, honest sleuthing, news-consumer tips and happy hell-raising with the powers-that-be to be found anywhere.

—**Molly Ivins**

Solomon is one of the sharpest media-watchers in the business.

—**Barbara Ehrenreich**

Demolishes the myth that liberalism dominates the media.

—**Doug Ireland**
The Nation

The charges are relentless, supported by facts and quotes, quite disturbing and uncomfortable—mighty welcome in these perilous merged-media times.

—**Patricia Holt**
San Francisco Chronicle

Do you get heartburn and indigestion when you read the incompetent, misdirected, same-old-crap, mainstream press? Are you seized with the impulse to destroy your TV set when you turn on Ted Koppel and see that he has Henry Kissinger as his guest for the 270th time? Relief for your condition is at hand...

—**Robert Sherrill**
The Texas Observer

OTHER BOOKS BY NORMAN SOLOMON

214-215 HINDENBURG talks with
SELDES !!
215 ~~EXCORIATED~~

The Habits of
Highly Deceptive Media

Decoding Spin and Lies
in Mainstream News

Norman Solomon

Common Courage Press   Monroe, Maine

Library of Congress Cataloging-in-Publication Data

Solomon, Norman, 1951–
   The habits of highly deceptive media : decoding spin and lies
in mainstream news / Norman Solomon.
        p.   cm.
   Includes index.
   ISBN 1-56751-155-4 (cloth). -- ISBN 1-56751-154-6 (pbk.)
   1. Journalism--Objectivity. 2. Mass media--Objectivity.
3. Journalistic ethics. 4. Mass media--Moral and ethical aspects.
I. Title
PN4784.024S655 1999
302.23--dc21   98-53040
                                                              CIP

Credits
   Cartoons by Matt Wuerker: Pages 10, 22, 37, 61, 165, 193, 231, 263
   Cartoons by Tom Tomorrow: Pages 32, 51, 77, 88, 102, 113, 257
   Cartoons on pages 14, 45 and 57 by Kirk Anderson, St. Paul, MN.
   Cartoons on pages 120, 179 and 197 by Clay Butler, Capitola, CA.
   Two pieces in this book—"Ménage à Trois: Cato, Murdoch,
Malone" and "Launching Pad for Authors: The Manhattan
Institute"—first appeared in *EXTRA!*, the magazine of the media
watch organization FAIR. (To subscribe, call 1-800-847-3993.)

Common Courage Press
Box 702
Monroe, ME 04951

www.commoncouragepress.com

207-525-0900   fax: 207-525-3068

First Printing

Contents

Part IV
Newspeaking

Part V
Maintaining the Punditocracy

Part VI
Deferring to Elites

Part XI
Fixating on Fame

Part XII
Worshipping Media Heroes, Old and New

Part XIII
Expelling Heretics From Media Temples

Part XIV
Shilling for Profitable Hypocrisy

Introduction

The tradition of Upton Sinclair, Lincoln Steffens, and I.F. Stone does not get much attention these days in the mainstream press, which may not be particularly eager to remember and extol its best-known critics; but that tradition is alive and well in this collection of courageously irreverent columns on the media by Norman Solomon.

Solomon's been bringing sharp analyses to the deceptions of the press for several years and he has never been afraid to take on the most powerful newspapers and most influential, and sometimes vindictive, television personalities. While others silence their dissent—or, in the more familiarly incestuous arrangements, manage to subdue it just enough to hold onto the favor of the powerful—Solomon plows fearlessly ahead.

The "deceptions" of the media alluded to by Solomon are not simply those that have to do with selectivity of sources or an obvious imbalance in the information offered, but also those more clever forms of media distortion that derive from subtle shadings in the use of words, the preferential use of favorable modifiers, and the calculated instruments of denigration.

One of the strangest myths of recent years has been the notion, frequently advanced by right-wing politicians, that the press tends to be liberal in its political opinions. Solomon gives this myth the heavy-duty demolition it deserves, pointing out how commonly—and comfortably—the press defends the interests of the privileged, how often stories that we read do little more than rubber-stamp the policy positions of extraordinarily conservative and influential think tanks, and how frequently the most prestigious sectors of the press identify so closely with the interests and the image and respectability of the United States in international affairs that they defend the indefensible when it is done by representatives or allies of our government.

Many of us, as we peruse newspapers, reach in irritation and impatience for a pen and start to decorate the margins with our furious rejoinders. Some of us old radicals hurl insults at our television sets. A few write angry letters to the press, which, if they're blunt enough to undercut an editor's most dearly held assumptions, are not likely to be published. Solomon writes the letters that we never wrote or did not have the nerve to mail. He fights the good fight without fear of consequence. He courts no favors. He writes responsibly and is meticulous on details, but he does not choke on false civility and brings a nicely sharpened scalpel and a good clear eye to sugar-coated contradictions.

The best critics of the press—the great dissenters—always did this. Thoreau did it. Garrison did it. Studs Terkel does it. Five generations of irreverent writers in *The Nation* did it, and still do it. Solomon's work is in that passionate tradition, which may not be good for high blood pressure but is absolutely crucial if we ever hope to have a truly free press in this democratic nation. All of us, including those whom he exposes and condemns the most severely, are indebted to him and should thank him for his courage.

Jonathan Kozol

Part I
Consolidating Media Power

If a TV News Anchor Talked Straight

Warren Beatty's movie *Bulworth* has caused quite a stir. The plot features a successful politician who begins to speak with absolute candor—a notion so outlandish that it's apt to sound incredible.

But the scenario might seem even more far-fetched if the film's blunt protagonist were a TV news anchor instead of a U.S. senator. Imagine how astonished you'd be if you turned on a television and found a newscast like this one:

"At the top of the news tonight—well, never mind. As usual, the script on my TelePrompTer is a scam. It's written to make money, not sense.

"Tonight, I'm supposed to say more about sorrow in the wake of the latest school tragedy. Yes, the sorrow is genuine. But the chances of your kid getting hit by a bullet at school are very small. During an average month in this country, four children die after being shot at school—while about 400 kids are killed by gunshots away from school grounds. Overall, poverty is a big risk factor.

"Meanwhile, television offers little to young people other than mediocre programs and a lot of commercials. As for TV news coverage: If it bleeds, it leads. But if it challenges social inequities, it rarely gets air time. We'd much rather run more footage of yellow police tape, grieving relatives and moralizing politicians.

"From the somber tone of some news stories, you might think that our network is appalled by violence. Don't make me laugh. This network adores violence. We broadcast plenty of it—in prime time—with guns often presented as the way to solve problems. And the conglomerate behind this network also owns a movie studio that puts out a continual stream of films glorifying murder and mayhem.

"During the last few years, White House conferences and newsmagazine covers have hailed scientific discoveries about the importance of the first years of a child's life. Duh. What did we think—that we could keep kicking kids around from year one and not have it affect them in crucial ways?

"While we've cheered the ascending stock market, children have seen us shortchanging their futures. I've been around long enough to know that lip service is meaningless compared to how we use our money.

"In many public schools, the students get little or no counseling—because, officials say, there's no money to hire more counselors. As for higher education, the Justice Policy Institute points out that government decision-makers 'have been robbing our universities to pay for prisons we don't need.'

"Back in 1995—while media outlets were busy distracting us with endless reports about O.J. Simpson—state governments made history by collectively spending more to build prisons than colleges. Prison construction went up by $926 million, to $2.6 billion, while university construction fell by $954 million, to $2.5 billion. How's that for planning a future for our kids?

"The Census Bureau recently found that 11.3 million Americans under age 19 had no health insurance (even though 92 percent of them had at least one working parent). Meanwhile, a study by the Center on Hunger, Poverty and Nutrition Policy at Tufts University calculated that more than 30 million Americans are going hungry—an increase of 50 percent since 1985.

"Today, among all the industrialized countries, the United States has the largest gap between rich and poor. But we're not going to spend much time talking about such facts on our newscasts. Why should we?

"It's not rocket science: To watch out for my career, I've kept a lid on—playing it safe—going along to get along with people more powerful than me. After all, I don't really work for journalists. I work for business executives. And the day I upset their apple cart is the day I'm looking at a pink slip with my name on it.

"Most of the news we put on television reminds me of the story about the emperor's new clothes—the royal guy parades around without a stitch on, but no one wants to take the risk of saying so out loud. Maybe you yell at your TV set. But believe me, the studio walls are just about soundproof. We can barely hear you. And we won't, unless you shout a whole lot louder."

May 27, 1998

Where the Media Momentum Is Headed

These days, many politicians are calling for campaign finance reform, but they keep raising as much cash as possible. Likewise, with less fanfare, journalists complain that their profession is turning into a money chase and they must keep pace.

Meanwhile, the media consumer resembles the proverbial frog in a pan of water—apt to be boiled to death before the gradual upturn of heat causes sufficient alarm. Accustomed to a steady rise in the degree of commercialization, few Americans take a leap toward active opposition.

Constant commercial intrusions—often laced with sexploitation—seem normal and acceptable because they're so routine in a wide array of media outlets. A lot of news reports are more akin to product promotion than journalism.

With cyberspace booming, it's difficult to predict exactly how media technology will change—the main guessing game for the industry analysts featured in mass media. They love to speculate about technical advances and fierce battles for market share.

But key questions get short shrift. Such as:

• In the future, will media coverage be diverse?

Prospects are bleak. Consolidation of media ownership has been so rapid in recent years that now just 10 corporations control most of this country's news and information flow. The top spot belongs to Time Warner, followed by Disney, Viacom, News Corporation (Rupert Murdoch), Sony, TCI, Seagram, Westinghouse, Gannett and General Electric.

Those conglomerates are in business to maximize profits. They're hardly inclined to provide much media space for advocates of curtailing their power.

- Who will have access to the glut of media programming?

For the most part, people who can pay for it.

Consider television. In most cases, the channels offered on cable TV are selected by big national cable-system firms that function as "gatekeepers." Not only is the range of programming limited—it's just available to viewers who can afford it. Basic cable service is liable to cost hundreds of dollars per year.

- Who will control the huge institutions running the mass-media show?

The brief answer is: millionaires and billionaires.

- Who will decide what news is important and what information should be widely disseminated?

In theory, journalists will. But, in practice, editors are accountable to media executives who, in turn, are accountable to top management.

- In the media nation on the horizon, what's democracy got to do with it?

The sad truth is likely to be: very little.

"Freedom of the press is guaranteed only to those who own one," critic A.J. Liebling quipped several decades ago. And now, of course, the presses are a small part of the news-media picture.

Already, just a few companies—including General Electric (which owns NBC), Westinghouse (CBS), Time Warner (CNN and cable systems), TCI (cable systems) and America Online—largely determine what makes it onto the screens we look at every day.

There's no sign that this trend is going to slow down. On the contrary, it has accelerated since the landmark Telecommunications Act became law in February 1996. Now, to a great extent, a few mammoth firms are programming America's media.

A hundred years ago, the writer Anatole France commented: "The law, in its majestic equality, forbids the rich as well as the poor to sleep under bridges, to beg in the streets, and to steal bread."

Today, a flip side of his observation is the fact that the federal government allows you and me, and billionaires like Rupert Murdoch, the right to buy as many newspapers, magazines, TV networks and satellite communication systems as we can.

The notion that a "free market" equals free speech is comforting but misleading—especially when a few bloated corporations have the economic weight to sit on the windpipe of the First Amendment.

If we get realistic about the obstacles blocking democratic discourse in our society, we can summon the determination to fight for the media diversity that future generations deserve.

October 15, 1997

Assessing Damages:
What About the Media?

Multibillion-dollar settlements have made big news lately. Some major industries are under pressure to admit the harm done by deceptive claims—such as ads about the joys of smoking or assurances about the safety of silicone breast implants.

Focusing on public health and product liability, the news coverage leaves the impression that the nation's media are innocent bystanders. But that's hardly the case.

Our society is dealing with dire consequences of the mass media's repeated messages and images. For instance:

- Many magazines and newspapers continue to publish full-page cigarette ads that glamorize smoking. But few media outlets do more than mention dry statistics on tobacco's effects.

How often have you seen grisly news photos or close-up TV footage of a smoker with an advanced stage of lung cancer? Or an in-depth story about what it's like to go through that illness?

- Although smoking has become less visible on television, it is now routine in many of the most widely marketed movies. According to a study at the University of California in San Francisco, half of the films put out from 1990 to 1995 showed a main character smoking—up from 29 percent during the 1970s.

Whether it's Julia Roberts in *My Best Friend's Wedding*, Brad Pitt in *Sleepers*, Arnold Schwarzenegger in *True Lies* or an angelic John Travolta in *Michael*, the big stars are puffing away—and the big movie studios are encouraging them to do so.

- Avid news readers and TV viewers are likely to learn more about Madonna's sex life than safe sex.

With rare exceptions, the mainstream media are still unwilling to provide detailed information about how to prevent AIDS. The same networks airing steamy prime-time TV scenes turn suddenly prudish when rejecting requests for straightforward public service spots about the proper use of a condom.

- For decades now, glorified images of svelte women have coincided with an epidemic of eating disorders. Media propaganda that equates thinness with desirability has a lot to do with the frequent occurrences of anorexia and bulimia among American girls and women. This, too, should be understood as a public health issue.

The media emphasis on stereotyped versions of beauty is pervasive. Who women are as people gets less attention than how they look. No wonder the self-esteem of so many girls plummets when they reach adolescence, with many destructive results.

- Children's TV programs include commercials that push soda pop and "energy drinks" heavily laden with sugar and caffeine. Ad campaigns for many other junk-food products also set a sugary hook for young consumers.

Years of denunciations have finally led to the announced retirement of cartoonish Joe Camel. But where are the demands to protect America's kids from the cute brand-name mascots that hawk everything from candy to beer?

- Sports events on television are especially thick with beer commercials, and neither TV networks nor local stations are balking. The woozy message is clear: People have a great time when they're drinking.

Some lavishly produced Budweiser ads feature youthful party-goers who appear to be well on their way to getting drunk. One personable young man crawls around on the floor searching for bottle caps that can be redeemed for neat prizes. It's a great promo for beer—and alcoholism.

What's really at stake here cannot be measured in monetary terms. The most severe damage has no price tag. Who among us knows no one affected by cigarette-linked cancer, serious eating disorders or heavy drinking? And how are we to count the costs?

No, the news media and the entertainment business aren't responsible for all those ills. But they are effectively promoting some major risk factors. And we're hearing very little acknowledgment of that grim reality.

August 27, 1997

And Now...
We're in "Media Jeopardy!"

Here's an all-new episode of "Media Jeopardy!"

You probably remember the rules: First, listen carefully to the answer. Then, try to come up with the correct question.

The first category is "Broadcast News."

- On ABC, CBS and NBC, the amount of TV network time devoted to this coverage has fallen to half of what it was during the late 1980s.

What is international news?

- A nationwide survey of 100 local TV newscasts in 55 cities, conducted by the Denver-based Rocky Mountain Media Watch, found that this topic is the lead story more often than all other subjects combined—and takes up one-third of the air time for news.

What is crime?

Now we move on to "Public Broadcasting."

- This public TV network, already airing several weekly shows hosted by conservatives such as William F. Buckley, John McLaughlin and Ben Wattenberg, is launching a new one-hour program called *National Desk*, which will feature a rotation of conservative hosts Fred Barnes, Larry Elder and Morton Kondracke.

What is PBS?

- It's the notion that PBS is a bastion of liberalism, despite the fact that the network's weekly lineup doesn't include a single public-affairs program hosted by a political progressive.

What is a media myth that will not die?

Our next category is "New Frontiers of Media Money."

- This daily satellite-TV feed has a captive audience of more than 8 million kids in classrooms. While it's touted as "a tool to educate and engage young adults in world happenings," the broadcast service sells commercials that go for nearly $200,000 per half-minute—pitched to advertisers as a way of gaining access to "the hardest-to-reach teen viewers."

What is Channel One?

- During the 1995–96 election cycle, these corporate parents of major networks gave a total of $3.2 million in "soft money" to the national Democratic and Republican parties.

Who are Disney (ABC), Time Warner (CNN), News Corporation (Fox), General Electric (NBC) and Westinghouse (CBS)?

- In 1996, this owner of the Fox TV network also donated $1 million, from his own pocket, to the California Republican Party.

Who is Rupert Murdoch?

- Eighteen months after the Walt Disney Company's 1995 purchase of the network where he's the main news anchor, this journalist cautiously told *Parade* magazine: "I feel, as any citizen, that more and more media in fewer hands, in the abstract, is reason to be concerned."

Who is Peter Jennings?

Now, it's on to "The End of Racism."

- A recent study of nightly news programs on the big three TV networks found that barely 1 percent of the stories were about people with this ethnic background (though they account for close to 15 percent of the U.S. public), and four-fifths of those rare stories focused on negative topics like crime and illegal immigration.

Who are Latinos?

- While they're about 25 percent of the U.S. population, a 1997 survey by the American Society of Newspaper Editors found that they comprise only 11.35 percent of the journalists in the newsrooms of this country's daily papers.

What are racial minorities?

We're moving into Media Double Jeopardy with our next category, "Fear and Favor."

- While this California newspaper was co-sponsoring a local amateur sporting event with Nike in the spring of 1997, top editors at the paper killed a staff columnist's article because it criticized Nike for rampant commercialism and use of overseas sweatshops.

What is the *San Francisco Examiner?*

- This seasoned United Press International reporter, who has worked on the presidential beat since the days of John F. Kennedy, says: "As long as I've covered the White House, there's been managed news. Secrecy is endemic in government."

Who is Helen Thomas?

- Back in 1983, when this book by journalist Ben Bagdikian first appeared, some critics called it "alarmist." Now hot-off-the-press in its fifth edition, the book documents that today just 10 corporations control most of this nation's newspapers, magazines, radio, TV, books and movies.

What is The Media Monopoly?

By now, we're in Serious Media Jeopardy.
No question about that.

June 18, 1997

When Coverage of Media Power Gets Hazy

Some people claim that large news outlets in the United States are refusing to acknowledge the dangers of centralized media ownership. But that's not quite true.

In mid-March [1997], a prominent *New York Times* article warned that "the lines between information and business are becoming increasingly blurred." The news story was blunt: "The concentration of power in the hands of a relative few— along with the linking of big money, big media and government power—has raised searching questions."

The newspaper reported that "critics say some media barons are out to protect their business interests and unfairly influence people."

Could it be that the *New York Times* is allowing its reporters to cover—without fear or favor—the massive consolidation of media control in this country?

Well, not exactly. The article quoted above was about news media in *Russia*.

Realists should not expect the *Times* to raise "searching questions" about its own inordinate power, which continues to grow.

In 1993, the New York Times Company bought one of the nation's few independent big-city dailies left, the *Boston Globe*. Now the company is greatly expanding daily delivery of the *Times* to newsstands and doorsteps all over the United States.

While some media firms rack up huge profits, others are merging or folding. The result is a dwindling number of media authorities who decide what news and opinions can reach the general public.

Fresh technologies might provide more space for media diversity. For instance, we've heard a lot lately about digital "high definition" television. But the federal government is giving away digital frequencies to corporate broadcasters.

In theory, the conventional airwaves—and the new digital frequencies—belong to the American public. In practice, these resources are in the pockets of those who could be described as "a relative few."

One day after publication of its alarming news story about media autocracy in Russia, the *Times* ran an editorial blithely endorsing the trend toward media autocracy here at home.

The *Times* encouraged the Federal Communications Commission to shower the broadcasting industry with free digital licenses. Meanwhile, a front-page *Wall Street Journal* report likened the digital TV spectrum to a "triple-layered banana split Uncle Sam is about to give the nation's broadcasters."

The *Journal* noted that "broadcasters would pay dearly to get those airwaves if they had to; estimates put their value at $20 billion to $50 billion. But the government is just days away from handing them over free of charge—and is asking for nothing in return."

Such transactions give new meaning to the term "the free market."

These giveaways are enriching outfits like the New York Times Company, a firm with annual revenues of $2.6 billion—and broadcast holdings that include several TV stations.

Adulation of "the free market" may be the closest thing to an official religion in this country. But, as usual with blind faith, the dominant theology gets lots of backing from profiteers.

Media worship of "the free market" is profuse and neverending. If you own the pulpits, you have quite a lot of say about what's preached—and assumed—on a daily basis. And heretics can rarely get a few words in edgewise.

That has been the case in recent media accounts of efforts to merge two office-supply chains. Many news stories echoed the full-page ads by Staples and Office Depot touting the benefits of a single superchain.

The Center for Study of Responsive Law analyzed the reporting in four key newspapers—the *New York Times*, *Washington Post*, *Wall Street Journal* and *USA Today*. The center found heavy reliance on statements from Staples and Office

Depot, "even though the claims made by these parties to the merger…were often wholly unsubstantiated."

What's more, "when they sought 'independent' comment, the major newspapers turned overwhelmingly to Wall Street analysts, many of whom have major financial stakes in the merger." Consumer advocates and specialists in antitrust law got short shrift.

In this merger-friendly atmosphere, what are the chances that big national news outlets will really scrutinize the anti-democratic effects of media consolidation in the United States? Somewhere between slim and zero.

It's far more likely that critical coverage of this disturbing U.S. media trend will appear in Russian newspapers.

March 19, 1997

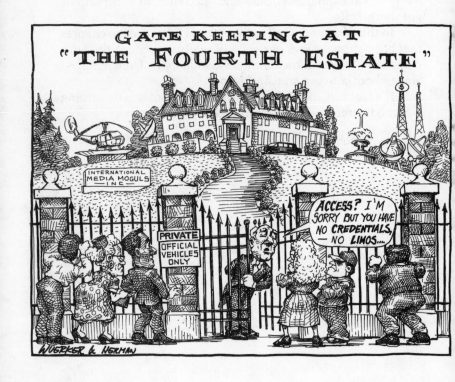

Part II
Shrugging Off Workers

What If We Didn't Need Labor Day?

Labor Day may be a fitting tribute to America's workers. But what about the other 364 days of the year? Despite all the talk about the importance and dignity of working people, they get little power or glory in the everyday world of news media.

What if the situation were reversed?

Once a year, big investors and corporate owners could be honored on Business Day. To celebrate the holiday, politicians might march arm in arm through downtown Manhattan with the likes of Bill Gates, Warren Buffett and Donald Trump. Executives could have the day off while media outlets said some nice things about them.

During the rest of the year, in this inverted scenario, journalists would focus on the real lives of the nation's workforce. Instead of making heroes out of billionaire investors—and instead of reporting on Wall Street as the ultimate center of people's economic lives—the news media would provide extensive coverage of the workplace.

For instance, such coverage would reflect the health hazards that workers face. On an average day, according to the Bureau of Labor Statistics, 17 Americans die from on-the-job injuries. Meanwhile, the daily rate of occupational injuries and illnesses in U.S. private industry is upwards of 18,350 people.

If media outlets can keep us so closely informed about stock prices every day, they could also keep us posted on exactly which industrial workplaces are killing and injuring America's workers. Much of the toll is less than obvious: Researchers have found that for each American killed by a workplace injury, another 10 or so job-related deaths occur due to disease.

If these grim events were reported on a daily basis, with the intensity and attention to detail now reserved for coverage of the stock market, then our society would be much more aware of working conditions across the country—and there would be more public pressure for improvement.

In a more labor-friendly media environment, televised punditry wouldn't be dominated by pro-corporate forums like *The Capital Gang, Hardball, The McLaughlin Group* and ABC's *This Week*—which, not coincidentally, are made possible by union-bashing firms like Archer Daniels Midland and General Electric. In contrast, prominent TV programs would present the outlooks of people who don't ride in limousines.

Public television—which now features shows like *Wall $treet Week* and *Nightly Business Report*—would find ways to air regular programs that might be called *Main Street Week* or *Nightly Labor Report*.

In this media dream world, National Public Radio would not have added a "business update" to its hourly news broadcasts. Or at least NPR would also be providing a "labor update" at the top of each hour.

The biggest-circulation daily paper in the country would not necessarily be the *Wall Street Journal*, a possession of Dow Jones & Company. Instead, it might be a newspaper owned by a coalition of labor unions. And the editorial pages would publish a real diversity of views.

On the magazine racks, periodicals like *Business Week* and *Forbes* (motto: "Capitalist Tool") would have to compete with equally bankrolled publications such as *Labor Week* and *Solidarity Forever* (motto: "Worker's Tool").

Congress would not get away with changing the name of Washington National Airport to Ronald Reagan National Airport, as occurred in February 1998. A pro-labor media atmosphere would make it politically untenable to name the airport after a former president who smashed the air traffic controllers' union early in his first term.

Not content to gush out a steady stream of platitudes about "democracy" and the "free market," the news media would probe the concept of workplace democracy.

Right now, the mass media rarely explore the idea of extending democratic principles to the institutions where

Americans work for a living. It's as though we've been conditioned to believe that our most exalted political values—free speech and the right to vote for the leaders of powerful institutions—should not intrude past the workplace door.

More than thirty years ago, satirist Tom Lehrer recorded a song about "National Brotherhood Week." "It's only for a week, so have no fear," he chortled. "Be grateful that it doesn't last all year!"

Labor Day lasts twenty-four hours. Too bad we need it.

September 2, 1998

Media to Americans:
You Never Had It So Good

The truth about America today depends on where you sit. And you probably don't sit in TV studios.

You may feel like you're working harder for less. Maybe you worry about medical coverage or job security or retirement. Maybe you're troubled by continuing signs of deterioration in many cities and towns.

If so, you're ignorant. For some time now, prominent news professionals have done their best to explain that you never had it so good.

The wise ones are trying to set you straight. This country is doing great. What you see every day may tell you different— but who are you going to believe, your two eyes or the most esteemed journalists in America?

If you sat in network TV studios on a regular basis, you'd be in a better position to appreciate the dazzling terrain of the Punditry Zone. The gamut runs from complacency to optimism.

Nothing in the news media epitomizes this zone more than *Washington Week in Review*. Airing on PBS television stations each Friday night, with several journalists talking around a table for half an hour, the program has a national audience of 3.2 million people.

Washington Week in Review began this year [1998] by letting viewers know just how contented they are.

"It's a different country, politically, than it was at the start of this decade," said David Broder of the *Washington Post*. "The level of anger is down. Frustration is less. When you go out and talk with people, they're just more ready to look at the hopeful side of things."

The main reason, Broder added, is the economy: "It has not 'raised all boats'…but it has certainly raised spirits for a lot of our fellow Americans." Minutes later, when *Los Angeles Times* reporter Ron Brownstein picked up the theme, he emphasized that "an awful lot of positive trends are coalescing suddenly in the cities."

Sitting at the same table seven days earlier, another *Washington Week in Review* regular, Alan Murray of the *Wall Street Journal*, was in similar high spirits as he hailed trickle-down affluence: "Inequality, which had gotten worse in the '70s and '80s, did start to get better in the last couple of years in spite of the stories you see about enormous CEO salaries and so forth. People at the bottom are moving up."

These days, many journalists sound like Broder, Brownstein and Murray. The echo effect is so loud that contrary information can barely be heard. Yet it's available.

At the Economic Policy Institute, a few miles from the *Washington Week in Review* studio, economist Jared Bernstein is well outside the Punditry Zone. "Low-wage workers have been taking it on the chin for two decades now," he told me. "Over the last year—thanks to tight labor markets, the increase in the minimum wage and low rates of inflation—they've gained back a bit of the ground they've lost. That doesn't mean the battle's over."

If the savants on *Washington Week* picked up the Jan. 12 [1998] issue of *The Nation* magazine, they'd find plenty of facts raining on their upbeat parade. For instance:

- "Poverty is increasing," *The Nation* reports. "The poverty rate last year, 13.7 percent, was higher than in 1989, despite seven years of nearly uninterrupted growth. Approximately 50 million Americans—19 percent of the population—live below the national poverty line."

- "The working poor are losing ground. In constant dollars, average weekly earnings for workers went from a high of $315 in 1973 down to $256 in 1996, a decline of 19 percent."

- "Income inequality is increasing. Last year, the poorest fifth of families saw their income decline by $210, while the richest 5 percent gained an average of $6,440 (not counting their capital gains)."

Silence about such facts surely doesn't bother top execs at Ford Motor Company, which has underwritten *Washington Week in Review* ever since 1979. Currently, Ford gives the program $1 million a year—nearly two-thirds of its entire budget.

A few days ago, Ford's chief executive announced that the company will soon post unprecedented figures for last year. "It is pretty clear now," he said, "that we will have a record year in terms of profits for 1997." Like many other huge firms, Ford never had it so good.

January 14, 1998

Adam Smith:
Too Left-Wing for the Networks?

Twenty reporters asked questions at Bill Clinton's news conference a few days ago [in early August 1997] on the White House lawn. One mentioned the nationwide UPS strike—and zinged the president for failing to intervene against the walkout.

"There are a lot of small businesses out there that are suffering right now as a result of this, and they see you standing by...not really doing anything about it," said CNN's Wolf Blitzer. He added: "Some of your critics are saying that's because the labor unions supported you and the Democrats so overwhelmingly."

Blitzer was echoing a familiar media tone. During a major strike, the damage to business is front-page news. But when workers are on the job, year in and year out, the adversity they face is a minor media matter.

We're all familiar with tributes to the dignity of working people. Many politicians and pundits are adept at such lofty rhetoric. But the media follow-through is quite uneven.

More than ever, big investors and top executives are on a pedestal. Typically, *Newsweek* began this month with a fawning cover story on "The New Rich." And it's not just a matter of news. Many ads glorify shrewd financiers and elite managers, portraying them as majestic creatures who soar above the rest of us.

Writer Thomas Frank has commented that many TV commercials now "star the noble businessman, striding in slow motion across the tarmac at sunset; standing with arms akimbo atop his skyscraper and surveying his domain; relaxing in business class as the thoughtful stewardess gently sees to his needs." The exalted exec is often shown "performing miracles of pie-chart transmission or conference-calling from some improbable place," whether a golf course or an igloo.

In sharp contrast, across the mass-media landscape, average workers hardly qualify as noble.

Daily papers and hourly news broadcasts keep us well informed of stock-market trends and outlooks for investors. But details aren't nearly as profuse when it comes to what directly affects most of the nation's employees: job-security issues, eroding benefits and stressful working conditions.

How often do we hear news updates on the extent of workplace safety? There would be plenty to report. A recent study published in the *Archives of Internal Medicine* found that the rate of work-related injuries and illnesses is 13.2 million Americans per year.

Meanwhile, media conglomerates are eager to curtail payrolls and benefits. So, for two years now in Detroit, 1,800 reporters and other newspaper workers have been on strike against the city's pair of dailies, owned by the huge Gannett and Knight-Ridder chains. This summer, a court ruling upheld charges that management engaged in unfair labor practices.

News accounts are apt to depict the "cost" of the work force as an impediment to wealth creation. But, way back in the 1770s, Adam Smith openly declared that labor creates all wealth: "It was not by gold or by silver, but by labor, that all the wealth of the world was originally purchased."

Smith was no champion of workers. One modern scholar calls him "the greatest of all conservative economists." Yet our country's journalistic tilt is so skewed that some of Adam Smith's key precepts would disqualify him from today's media mainstream.

In *The Wealth of Nations*, published 221 years ago, Smith wrote with realism about manufacturers and merchants. He described them as "men whose interest is never exactly the same with that of the public, who have generally an interest to deceive and even to oppress the public, and who accordingly have, upon many occasions, both deceived and oppressed it."

Talk like that is a real turn-off for the producers who decide which political analysts belong on national television.

PREDICTABLY, MUCH COVERAGE OF THE UPS STRIKE WAS SLANTED TOWARD THE STATUS QUO...SOME CORRESPONDENTS ACTUALLY CHASTISED THE PRESIDENT FOR *NOT* INTERVENING ON BEHALF OF MANAGEMENT...

SIR--WHY HAVEN'T YOU CRACKED DOWN ON THESE *DISRUPTIVE TROUBLE-MAKERS*--

--AND SQUASHED THEM LIKE *COCK-ROACHES*?!

ER--I--AH--

OF COURSE, LABOR HAS BEEN SO THOROUGHLY *MARGINALIZED* IN THIS COUNTRY, MANY COMMENTATORS' ONLY FRAME OF REFERENCE SEEMED TO BE THE *BASEBALL* WALKOUT...

THE PUBLIC WAS LESS SYMPATHETIC TO THE MILLIONAIRE BALL-PLAYERS, BIFF!

I WONDER WHAT THE *DIFFERENCE* IS! AFTER ALL--A *STRIKE* IS A *STRIKE*, RIGHT?

THE NEW YORK TIMES REPORTED WITH SURPRISE THAT (ACCORDING TO THEIR POLL) 55% OF AMERICANS BACKED THE STRIKERS...THOUGH FRANKLY, WE WERE MORE SURPRISED THAT A FULL 27% SIDED WITH *UPS*...

THEIR PROFIT MARGINS ARE *SURE* TO *SUFFER*!

DAMN THOSE UNION THUGS!

NEW WACKY MEAL $1.99

AFTER ALL, IN AN ERA OF WIDESPREAD *WAGE STAGNATION* AND *DOWNSIZING*...WELL, IT DOESN'T TAKE A *ROCKET SCIENTIST* TO UNDERSTAND THAT *UNIONS* ARE NOT THE *PROBLEM* HERE, FOLKS...

HEY-- *THIS* COMPANY IS LIKE A *BIG HAP-PY FAMILY*--RIGHT, SON?

UH, SURE BOSS...

...ONE THAT HAS TO *BUMP OFF* AN EXTRA *COUSIN* OR TWO OCCASIONALLY...

TOM TOMORROW © 9-3-97

Could Adam Smith get a job as a network TV pundit to talk about economic issues today? Would he be allowed to host a weekly PBS program on the economy? I doubt it. Too left-wing.

August 6, 1997

Great News:
Your Wages Aren't Going Up

April [1997] ended with some very good news: Wages are stagnant.

If you work for a living, that may sound a bit odd. But for the news media, it makes perfect sense to claim that what's bad for workers is good for the economy.

So, the April 30 front page of the *New York Times* trumpeted the latest economic news with a cheery headline—"Markets Surge as Labor Costs Stay in Check."

"The stock market rocketed yesterday to its greatest gain in more than five years," the *Times* reported. Why? Because important people were happy that wages had barely increased in the United States. And employers hadn't shelled out more for "benefits like health insurance and pensions."

The *Times* front page spotlighted the jubilant comment of a senior economist at the huge brokerage firm of Goldman, Sachs and Company: "There is no question this is a better labor cost report than we had anticipated."

"Better" for employers. But how about workers? Well, they're not worth much ink. And they're certainly not worth hearing. The 18-paragraph *Times* article quoted a few current and former government economists—without a word from workers, their representatives or labor advocates.

When more money is in our pay envelopes, many news reports tell us that's bad. It's "inflationary," and it means that the economy is "overheating." But when stocks and bonds soar in value, that's supposed to make us all feel good about economic progress.

News outlets often seem dazzled by Wall Street. That fascination is intense on public television, where programs like the *Nightly Business Report* and Louis Rukeyser's *Wall $treet Week* keep close tabs on stock-market trends.

Catering to an upscale audience, public TV depends on millions of dollars from major companies pleased to "underwrite" programming that promotes their outlooks. It shouldn't surprise us that the *NewsHour With Jim Lehrer*—funded by an agribusiness giant and an insurance company—devotes long and fervent segments to the stock market.

The media emphasis has gotten so out of whack that we're encouraged to care more about the fortunes of Wall Street than the incomes on our own street.

But only 2 percent of the public owns half of the country's individual stock and bond holdings. Other people in the market are very small investors. And 80 percent of Americans have no direct stake in the stock markets at all. (Employees with indirect holdings via pension funds have no say in how the money is invested and can't get access to proceeds until they retire.)

Although most news accounts leave the vague impression that an upswing in the stock market augurs well for the nation's work force, the opposite has been the case.

For nearly a quarter of a century, despite advances in education, the picture for America's workers has been bleak. During that time, real wages for males have dropped 15 percent. And while women have entered a wider range of jobs, their real wages have increased by only 4 percent.

Meanwhile, investor gains and corporate profits went through the roof. Government macroeconomic policies have served Wall Street's interests—while flattening workers' income.

Just as evidence of wage stagnation makes stocks rise, Wall Streeters are frequently ecstatic to learn that a major corporation has decided to slash its payroll. "Downsizing" usually sends stock prices climbing.

Clearly, big-money investors and average workers have very different interests. But anyone who points that out is liable to face media attack for encouraging class warfare.

Actually, the mass media don't seem to mind the class warfare that's continually waged from the top down—undermining the economic security of workers in the name of streamlining production.

"Sacred though jobs allegedly are, the institutions that have been eliminating them by the scores of thousands for their own private profit advantage are never condemned for this in mainstream comment," writes economist Edward S. Herman. "They are even complimented for having taken steps to improve efficiency, productivity and 'competitiveness.' "

Herman is professor emeritus at the University of Pennsylvania's esteemed Wharton School. But he's out of step with the news media because he is much too concerned about the well-being of workers: "The euphemisms, including 'purr' words like restructuring and efficiency, divert attention from the fact that human lives are being shattered."

The news media are absolutely bullish on Wall Street. But workers remain undervalued—and suffer the consequences.

April 30, 1997

Part III
Giving Short Shrift to the Poor

Going Hungry:
News That Really Matters

Two days after many TV networks aired every moment of Bill Clinton's grand-jury testimony, several members of Congress teamed up with researchers and activists for a dramatic forum about "economic human rights." The independent hearing focused on matters of profound importance—and the big news media ignored it.

The gathering took place on Capitol Hill, right under the noses of the Washington press corps. And the media establishment stayed away in droves. Not a single TV camera was there. In fact, hardly any journalists showed up.

"Thirty million Americans are hungry," notes the Institute for Food and Development Policy, also known as Food First, which helped to organize the Sept. 23 [1998] forum. Somewhere between five million and seven million are homeless. "More than forty million Americans have no health insurance. And the country has the highest rate of child poverty among the industrialized countries."

The institute emphasizes that "hunger is not an accident, in the U.S. or anywhere else. There is no scarcity of food in the world. Certainly there's no shortage here in America." Yet, "the number of hungry people in America has increased by half since 1985."

While we keep being told that the nation's economy is robust, inequities continue to widen. "Sure, there are more millionaires than ever in the U.S.," says Food First. "But for every new millionaire, there are countless new hungry people for whom $100 or $200 a month in food stamps is the only safeguard against malnutrition, even starvation."

So, why don't we hear more about hunger in the United States? A key factor is the media industry's fixation on demographics. "Because the mass media is aimed at the people with the highest disposable income, we see pictures of hunger overseas, but not our own," Food First observes. "Perhaps that's a reason why the growth of the Hunger Class has been ignored politically."

The forum on economic human rights included testimony from scholars. But there were also firsthand accounts of being hungry in America. "It isn't that I never worked," said a grandmother named Katherine Engles. "I worked since I was 14 years old. The jobs that are out there—you are not making enough in order to live. Mothers go hungry at night so their children can eat."

In the glazed-over eyes of editors in Washington, her words were not significant. But they remain: "When you are hungry, it's really hard. Sometimes, I would psyche myself to a cup of tea and try to make myself feel as though I just ate a full-course meal even though I didn't. Sometimes, I would roll bread up into little dough balls to try to fill myself up. It gets to a point where you kind of get used to it. Till today, I can't eat no more than one meal a day. It's what I am used to, and even today it's about all we can afford anyway."

And, she added: "I keep looking at the bigger issue. What's ahead for our children, our grandchildren? What is ahead for them?"

Engles was one of 200 people, many of them poor, who filled the room in the Rayburn House Office Building to support a "Fairness Agenda for America." The media odds were stacked against them—and not only because of the frenzy over President Clinton and Monica Lewinsky.

Major media outlets have usually stayed away from efforts to challenge economic disparities. Traditional news judgment dictates that journalists tread lightly on the subject of who really wields the economic power—and at whose expense—in the United States.

(Although media gatekeepers blocked the recent forum in Washington, plenty of information is available—at www.food-first.org and www.netprogress.org—on the Web.)

People fighting for economic human rights have always had an uphill battle for space in the mass media. Now, the media terrain is tilted against them more than ever.

Can you imagine what would have happened this year if the news media concentrated on hunger in America with the same fierce determination that has pervaded coverage of sex near the Oval Office? By now, life would be much better for a lot of children who will go to bed hungry tonight.

September 23, 1998

Only Some Babies Dazzle News Media

When Bobbi McCaughey gave birth to septuplets, she became an instant heroine. Fame and fortune arrived with her babies. The news media went nuts. And the gifts poured in.

It's been one heck of a baby shower. In the words of the Associated Press, the seven McCaughey infants "have received, among other things, a free van, groceries for a year, a lifetime supply of diapers, college scholarships and free cable for seven years—one year for each baby."

Newsweek's special contribution came in the form of free dental work on its cover, where the smiling mom's teeth were straightened and whitened by computer. A spokeswoman for the magazine later conceded that "perhaps" the photo technicians "reconstructed too much."

A few days after the McCaughey family boosted Iowa's population by seven, the news broke that a mother who gave birth to six babies earlier in the year had not fared nearly as well. Jacqueline Thompson, the first black woman with sextuplets born in the United States, was living in obscurity as she struggled to raise her children in Washington, D.C.

The disparity between the McCaugheys' fame and the Thompsons' oblivion surfaced just before Thanksgiving. Suddenly, the hard-working mother and her blue-collar husband were buoyed by a flash flood of charity. General Motors gave the Thompson clan a minivan—for presentation on a nationally syndicated TV show. A Ford dealer came up with a slightly used blue Aerostar.

In recent days, plenty of baby clothes, diaper-rash ointment, teething gel and strollers have arrived, along with a lot of small checks. A foundation set up by a mortgage investor announced that it will give the Thompsons a house.

While such generosity is all well and good, it's very likely the media interest and the public response would have come much sooner for the Thompson newborns if they'd been white.

That kind of tacit racism is only one of the problems with the media's mania for multiple births.

In this country, thousands of babies are born into dire poverty each week—and the news media commonly depict their mothers as problematic rather than heroic. Evidently, if a low-income mom gives birth to half-a-dozen babies at once, she merits journalistic concern and strong community support. But if she gives birth to several babies one at a time, she's apt to be seen as an intractable social problem.

Politicians and media pundits often speak as though the typical beleaguered mother with scant income doesn't deserve much of anything. She certainly doesn't get her teeth whitened or straightened on any magazine covers.

While *Newsweek* was putting the finishing retouches on Bobbi McCaughey's teeth, the London-based *Financial Times* reported a grim story on its front page, under the headline "Reform May Push U.S. Poor Into Squalor."

The article was blunt: "Large numbers of Americans risk destitution when the law requiring people on welfare to take jobs comes fully into effect 18 months from now." Citing the results of a national survey by the U.S. Conference of Mayors, the newspaper sketched a bleak picture.

"A key problem was that welfare recipients were heavily concentrated in inner cities when vast numbers of retail and low-skill jobs had migrated to suburban shopping malls and industrial parks," the *Financial Times* said. "Public transport did not reach them and most welfare recipients lacked cars."

Of course, few of the low-income parents in such situations will be receiving free minivans.

As for medical care, there's more bad news: The mayors estimate that only 27 percent of "low skill" jobs offer health insurance. For many families, when welfare disappears, so will health coverage. Meanwhile, child-care subsidies are so meager that mothers with young children often have few realistic options for working outside the home.

The news media can be very effective at showing us what's poignant and laudable about one family with limited resources.

But the focus gets hazy when considering millions of those families: The coverage tends to become quite abstract.

Eager to report on upbeat examples of generosity, numerous stories about septuplets and sextuplets tell us that our society is committed to taking care of children. Maybe we're trying to convince ourselves, despite all the evidence to the contrary.

November 26, 1997

THE PRESS CONTINUES TO COVER THE HOMELESS

Media "Peep Show"
Gawks at the Poor

News coverage of poverty in America has become a peep show. Every day, poor people are on display as victims of misfortune or victimizers of each other: Step right up and take a look at violence, drug abuse and despair.

Media peepholes allow the public to see some lurid effects of widespread poverty in this land of plenty. But the range of sight is so narrow that even the better coverage gets jammed into a woefully inadequate frame.

A case in point is *Remorse*, the National Public Radio documentary that just won the grand prize of the 1997 Robert F. Kennedy Journalism Awards. With the help of NPR producers, two black teenagers assembled a moving audio portrait of life and death in their Chicago housing project.

The one-hour documentary, which aired on the *All Things Considered* program, was creative. Yet NPR's role leaves a bad odor. The problem is context: NPR News rarely explores how powerful elites benefit from—and perpetuate—chronic poverty.

That avoidance is routine. The mass media dodge the basic inequities that mean great profits for some and great misery for many others. Mainstream outlets don't shed light on how investors and faceless corporations keep feeding their bottom lines at the expense of America's poor.

A lot of people abhor this status quo—which has a clear racial component. While poverty afflicts millions of whites, it falls disproportionately on blacks, Latinos and Native Americans. But media peepholes exclude a full view of such realities.

In fact, days before NPR put out a press release to announce the RFK Journalism Award, *All Things Considered* censored a two-minute poem making a strong statement about some current manifestations of power and racism.

In the past, *All Things Considered* has aired a number of poems by Martín Espada. Three years ago, the program commissioned what became the title poem of his book *Imagine the Angels of Bread*. Soon after it won the American Book Award this spring [1997], *All Things Considered* asked him to write a poem for broadcast in connection with National Poetry Month.

Espada wrote a poem about Mumia Abu-Jamal, a journalist and black activist who is on death row after being convicted of the murder of a Philadelphia police officer. While alluding to evidence of an unfair trial, the poem lyrically evokes "fugitive slaves" and a history of racial oppression spanning to the present time.

NPR refused to air the poem. Evidently, the last thing NPR's management wanted to do was rile the formidable police lobby, which went ballistic in 1994 when *All Things Considered* scheduled a series of commentaries by Abu-Jamal about crime and prison life. NPR quickly canceled the commentaries.

Now, NPR has also banned poems about Abu-Jamal.

NPR's director of communications, Kathy Scott, told me that the poem has been blocked for the same reason that Abu-Jamal's original commentaries were axed: pending litigation.

Using a rationale without legal basis, Scott asserted that the problem with the poem is a lawsuit filed by Abu-Jamal against NPR for canceling his commentaries. And, she claimed, the problem with those commentaries was Abu-Jamal's appeal of his death sentence: NPR's intention was to "not influence the case so that the legal system can take its course."

So, once Abu-Jamal's case is settled, perhaps by execution, NPR's ban on his voice might be lifted.

On the phone from the University of Massachusetts in Amherst, where he's an associate professor, Espada sounded calm—and disgusted. He recalled his question to an NPR producer: "NPR is refusing to air this poem because of its political content. Do you agree?" The answer was yes.

James Baldwin once wrote that many people who live with complicity in the destruction of other human beings "do not know it and do not want to know it." He added: "But it is not permissible that the authors of devastation should also be innocent. It is the innocence which constitutes the crime."

For news coverage to keep the public "innocent," the peep show must go on.

May 14, 1997

Motherhood, Apple Pie
and "Volunteerism"

Get ready for a heavy dose of hoopla about "volunteerism" at the end of this month [April 1997], when we'll be seeing profuse media coverage of the Presidents' Summit for America's Future.

For Bill Clinton, the summit in Philadelphia—which he's co-hosting with George Bush—is the political equivalent of a slam dunk. Fervent appeals for volunteers to save our young people are sure to generate plenty of cheers.

With 2,000 delegates expected from around the country, the White House assumes that the news media will treat the spectacle with apple-pie reverence. After all, only a nitwit doubts that Americans should go out of their way to help each other.

We've been here before. Remember President Bush's "Thousand Points of Light"?

Near the close of the 1980s—with much of the nation reeling from "trickle-down" economics that subsidized the rich and undermined the rest of us—Bush launched a major rhetorical drive to promote voluntary good deeds.

Countless news stories boosted the volunteer theme. Typical was a *Christian Science Monitor* article published in November 1989 under the headline "A Thousand Points of Light to Shine."

The *Monitor* breathlessly reported that Bush "will be asking every commercial establishment to join voluntarily in efforts to find solutions for such problems as illiteracy, dropouts, drug abuse, unwed-teen pregnancy, youth delinquency and suicide, AIDS, homelessness, hunger, unemployment and loneliness."

Then, as now, the man in the Oval Office was anxious to have it both ways—cutting back on government aid to people in need while posing as a champion of compassion. In a country ablaze with grave crises, that's like the fire chief urging everyone to fill their squirt guns.

Volunteerism is admirable. Across the United States, it involves many sincere people who want to help others. But it's no substitute for dependable, ongoing, government-funded programs with adequate budgets.

Not a single officeholder in America would dream of depending on volunteerism to sustain local police departments. But somehow we're supposed to believe that hit-or-miss, woefully underfunded charity efforts are central to meeting the most basic human needs.

Reliance on volunteerism means that the unfortunate in our society will remain at the mercy of the ebb and flow of meager charitable resources. This has been going on for a very long time.

In retrospect—despite the prodigious output of media blather and the abundant hot air from the Bush White House—the thousand points of light were no match for the nation's millions of points of blight.

Hardly a slacker when it comes to mobilizing behind hollow slogans, President Clinton now delights in pounding the bully pulpit for volunteerism. Rather than fighting to fulfill New Deal principles with strong federal programs for social uplift, he preaches that everyone should be a volunteer.

Clinton lauds volunteerism as "the very American idea that we can meet our challenges, not through heavy-handed government or as isolated individuals, but as members of a true community—all of us working together." Such words are cold comfort.

For politicians and journalists alike, the great allure of volunteerism is that it seems to transcend political differences, leaving ideology behind. It's good—period.

But proclaiming that volunteerism can overcome deep-rooted social ills is profoundly ideological. It's the rough equivalent of telling people that they should figure out how to fix crumbling roads and bridges themselves, rather than expect help from the government.

BY NOW, YOU'VE UNDOUBTEDLY BEEN INUNDATED WITH UPLIFTING BANALITIES ABOUT--AND HEARTWARMING EXAMPLES OF-- *VOLUNTEERISM* ...

I'M HOLDING A BAKE SALE TO END WORLD HUNGER!

I'M TRYING TO CURE *AIDS* WITH MY *JUNIOR SCIENTIST CHEMISTRY LAB!*

I'M HOSTING A *COCKTAIL PARTY* TO SAVE THE *OZONE LAYER!*

WE HATE TO BE CONTRARIANS HERE,* BUT AREN'T PROBLEMS LIKE THESE--LARGE, OVERWHELMING PROBLEMS THAT NO ONE PERSON CAN SOLVE ALONE-- AREN'T THESE THE VERY *RAISON D'ÊTRE* OF GOVERNMENT? AND ISN'T THE PROMOTION OF *VOLUNTEERISM* AS A SOLUTION TO SUCH PROBLEMS JUST AN EASY WAY TO COMPENSATE FOR ILL-CONSIDERED *BUDGET CUTS?*

HEH, HEH... YOU FOLKS WORRY ABOUT HOMELESSNESS, TEEN PREGNANCY AND DRUG ABUSE--

--AND *WE'LL* WORRY ABOUT THE *V-CHIP!*

AND KEN STARR.

*NO WE DON'T.

CHURCHES AND PRIVATE CHARITIES JUST DON'T HAVE THE *RESOURCES* TO REPLACE PUBLICLY FUNDED SOCIAL PROGRAMS-- AND WHY SHOULD THEY BE *EXPECTED* TO? HAVE OUR SOCIETAL PRIORITIES REALLY GROWN SO *TWISTED* THAT WE'D RATHER CAST THE NEEDY TO THE *WOLVES* THAN SPEND ANY MORE *MONEY* ON THEM?

WELL, IN A WORD...

...YES.

MODERN TIMES
PREZ TO POOR: EAT CAKE!

DON'T GET US WRONG; WE APPLAUD THE IMPULSE TO VOLUNTEER... WE JUST HATE TO SEE IT *ABUSED* BY A GOVERNMENT SHIRKING ITS *SIMPLEST RESPONSIBILITIES...*

WELL, THAT'S THE LAST POTHOLE ON *ORANGE STREET!*

OKAY-- LET'S MOVE UP TO *LIVINGSTON!*

ISN'T IT WONDERFUL TO FEEL LIKE YOU'RE *DOING* YOUR PART?

CEMENT

TOM TOMORROW © 5-7-97

The Summit for America's Future—featuring retired General Colin Powell as well as Clinton and former presidents—is bound to get big media play. But it promises to be much ado about next to nothing. In essence, Clinton and other summit leaders are fiddling with easy rhetoric while social problems burn.

Instead of harmonizing with facile platitudes, the news media should be asking some tough questions about the political emphasis on volunteerism. So far, that hasn't happened.

April 9, 1997

Part IV
Newspeaking

Orwellian Logic 101—
A Few Simple Lessons

When U.S. missiles hit sites in Sudan and Afghanistan, some Americans seemed uncomfortable. A vocal minority even voiced opposition after the attacks in late August [1998]. But approval was routine among those who had learned a few easy Orwellian lessons.

When terrorists attack, they're terrorizing. When we attack, we're retaliating. When they respond to our retaliation with further attacks, they're terrorizing again. When we respond with further attacks, we're retaliating again.

When people decry civilian deaths caused by the U.S. government, they're aiding propaganda efforts. In sharp contrast, when civilian deaths are caused by bombers who hate America, the perpetrators are evil and those deaths are tragedies.

When they put bombs in cars and kill people, they're uncivilized killers. When we put bombs on missiles and kill people, we're upholding civilized values.

When they kill, they're terrorists. When we kill, we're striking against terror.

At all times, Americans must be kept fully informed about who to hate and fear. When the United States found Osama bin Laden useful during the 1980s because of his tenacious violence against the Soviet occupiers in Afghanistan, he was good, or at least not bad—but now he's really bad.

No matter how many times they've lied in the past, U.S. officials are credible in the present. When they vaguely cite evidence that the bombed pharmaceutical factory in Khartoum was making ingredients for nerve gas, that should be good enough for us.

Might doesn't make right—except in the real world, when it's American might. Only someone of dubious political orientation would split hairs about international law.

When the mass media in some foreign countries serve as megaphones for the rhetoric of their government, the result is ludicrous propaganda. When the mass media in our country serve as megaphones for the rhetoric of the U.S. government, the result is responsible journalism.

Unlike the TV anchors spouting the government line in places like Sudan and Afghanistan, ours don't have to be told what to say. They have the freedom to report as they choose.

"Circus dogs jump when the trainer cracks his whip," George Orwell observed, "but the really well-trained dog is the one that turns his somersault when there is no whip."

Orwell noted that language "becomes ugly and inaccurate because our thoughts are foolish, but the slovenliness of our language makes it easier for us to have foolish thoughts." And his novel *1984* explained that "the special function of certain Newspeak words…was not so much to express meanings as to destroy them."

National security. Western values. The world community. War against terrorism. Collateral damage. American interests.

What's so wondrous about Orwellian processes is that they tend to be very well camouflaged—part of the normal scenery. Day in and day out, we take them for granted. And we're apt to stay away from uncharted mental paths.

In *1984*, Orwell wrote about the conditioned reflex of "stopping short, as though by instinct, at the threshold of any dangerous thought…and of being bored or repelled by any train of thought which is capable of leading in a heretical direction."

Orwell described "doublethink" as the willingness "to forget any fact that has become inconvenient, and then, when it becomes necessary again, to draw it back from oblivion for just so long as it is needed."

In his afterword to *1984*, Erich Fromm emphasized "the point which is essential for the understanding of Orwell's book, namely that 'doublethink' is already with us, and not merely something which will happen in the future, and in dictatorships."

Fifty-two years ago, Orwell wrote an essay titled "Politics and the English Language." Today, his words remain as relevant as ever: "In our time, political speech and writing are largely the defense of the indefensible."

Repression and atrocities "can indeed be defended," Orwell added, "but only by arguments which are too brutal for most people to face, and which do not square with the professed aims of political parties. Thus political language has to consist largely of euphemism, question-begging and sheer, cloudy vagueness."

National security. Western values. The world community. War against terrorism. Collateral damage. American interests.

August 26, 1998

Retractions of Reporting
Are Quite Selective

Judging from the uproar about recent retractions by CNN and *Time* magazine, you might conclude that American journalism maintains high standards for war-related reporting—and sets the record straight when those standards aren't met. But nothing could be farther from the truth.

Early this month [July 1998], under enormous pressure, CNN and *Time* retracted their joint reports in June that said the U.S. military used nerve gas against American defectors in Laos during the Vietnam War. But it would be a big mistake to assume that inaccurate stories get retracted.

News accounts routinely serve as conveyor belts for dubious information from high-ranking officials in Washington. Those sources, often unnamed, are apt to provide self-serving mixtures of facts and falsehoods.

But if no one in a powerful position raises a squawk, then there's rarely any pressure for a correction, much less a retraction. On the contrary, officials are appreciative of a story—however untrue—if it moves their agendas forward.

That's how lies can routinely be reported as truth—with tragic consequences.

Here's a momentous example: For a third of a century, U.S. media outlets have not bothered to retract their false reporting of events in the Gulf of Tonkin.

On Aug. 5, 1964, American news media reported that North Vietnamese forces—for the second time in three days—had launched unprovoked attacks on U.S. ships in the Tonkin Gulf.

Across the United States, front pages presented fabrications as facts. The *New York Times* proclaimed that the U.S. government was retaliating "after renewed attacks against American destroyers in the Gulf of Tonkin." The *Washington Post*'s headline told of a "Second Attack on Our Destroyers."

Two days later, the Gulf of Tonkin Resolution—the closest thing there ever was to a declaration of war against North Vietnam—gained nearly unanimous approval from Congress. The resolution authorized the president "to take all necessary measures to repel any armed attack against the forces of the United States and to prevent further aggression."

But the attack by North Vietnam on Aug. 2 wasn't "unprovoked." And the "second attack" never occurred.

As months became years and then decades, major U.S. media outlets still didn't issue a retraction.

This summer, I asked a number of *Washington Post* staffers whether the newspaper ever retracted its Tonkin Gulf reporting. Finally, the trail led to someone with a definitive answer.

"I can assure you that there was never any retraction," said Murrey Marder, a reporter who wrote much of the *Washington Post*'s coverage of August 1964 events in the Gulf of Tonkin. He added: "If you were making a retraction, you'd have to make a retraction of virtually everyone's entire coverage of the Vietnam War."

Marder remembers that the U.S.-backed South Vietnamese navy had been shelling North Vietnamese coastal islands just prior to the reported attacks by North Vietnam on U.S. ships in the Tonkin Gulf. But the propaganda machinery was in high gear: "Before I could do anything as a reporter, the *Washington Post* had endorsed the Gulf of Tonkin Resolution."

The news coverage of events in the Tonkin Gulf "was all driven by the White House," recalled Marder, who was a *Post* reporter from 1946 to 1985. "It was an operation—a deliberate manipulation of public opinion... None of us knew, of course, that there had been drafted, months before, a resolution to justify American direct entry into the war, which became the Gulf of Tonkin Resolution."

Marder commented: "If the American press had been doing its job and the Congress had been doing its job, we would never have been involved in the Vietnam War."

Since then, U.S. forces invaded Grenada and Panama in the 1980s and made war on Iraq in the 1990s. Less-direct intervention from Washington, in Central America and elsewhere, also took many lives. In the process, quite a few journalists enhanced their careers by more or less telling the favorite stories of the Pentagon, the State Department and the White House.

Reliance on official sources has remained a routine part of news coverage. And the biggest problems with American journalism still include stories that never get retracted.

July 8, 1998

The Disturbing Eagerness
for a Bloody Attack

After Saddam Hussein's pledge of full cooperation with U.N. weapons inspectors led President Clinton to cancel air attacks at the last minute in mid-November [1998], a strong wave of frustration swept through American news media.

The pattern was all too familiar, the refrain went. Yet again, the U.S. government ended up taking yes for an answer from Iraq's cunning despot.

Many commentators griped about the cost of mobilizing and then not attacking. Each time the United States sends a fleet to the Persian Gulf, the buildup costs another $1 billion or so. What good is repeated deployment of enormous firepower if it isn't used?

Quite a few pundits sounded very disappointed—as if a long-desired ice cream cone was near their lips and then went splat on the sidewalk.

Two days after President Clinton proclaimed that "Iraq has backed down," the *Washington Post* filled its opinion page with caustic reactions from three prominent syndicated columnists.

Clinton again proved that he's a wimp, George Will observed from the front lines of his word processor. The commentator warned against restraint: "U.S. forces should quickly destroy any site, such as a presidential compound, that inspectors are prevented from examining."

Meanwhile, Charles Krauthammer wrote that "Clinton was given an extraordinary opportunity to strike a massive blow against Saddam. He flinched." Krauthammer briefly noted that "the military's estimate of casualties from an initial strike" was "10,000 Iraqi dead"—but who cares? Uncle Sam should strive to "disarm, disrupt and destroy Saddam's regime. A relentless air campaign had a good chance of doing that."

Liberal Richard Cohen was not to be outdone in the blood-thirst department. "Both countries backed down—one the world's only superpower, the other a Third World country, short of everything but gall," he declared. "Something is out of balance here. The Clinton administration waited too long to act. It needed to punch out Iraq's lights, and it did not do so."

Hypocrisy abounds, but never mind that. With U.S. support, Israel has violated numerous U.N. resolutions while maintaining its occupations of the West Bank and Gaza as well as southern Lebanon. Running weapons facilities that have produced about 200 nuclear warheads, Israel still refuses to allow any international inspection.

The United States invokes the sanctity of the United Nations when useful but ignores that world body whenever convenient—and reserves the right to unilaterally attack Iraq whether the U.N. likes it or not.

Often, the paramount U.S. media concerns have been framed in macho terms. Recent news coverage focused on a question that led off a front-page *New York Times* article: "Who blinked?" Many American journalists lamented that Clinton did not entirely stare down Saddam Hussein.

The *New York Post* scornfully editorialized that Clinton had not been able to "act like a man." The newspaper, owned by Rupert Murdoch, added that "whenever circumstances have demanded that this president rise to the occasion and really be president, he has failed the United States and the world."

Frustrated as they were by the lack of military consummation, cable TV networks and other media outlets were soon able to replace the faded specter of a bloody high-tech assault with audio recordings of Linda Tripp and Monica Lewinsky.

Of course, the telephone tapes couldn't quite be touted as new—the printed transcripts had been released several weeks earlier—but more nuances were available. The Associated Press echoed the widespread hype by reporting that the twenty-two hours of tapes "gave America its first chance to hear Ms. Lewinsky's voice." AP explained that "what was new Tuesday was the emotion and inflection."

And so it goes. "Emotion" is supposed to matter greatly in some contexts. In others, such as past and future U.S. missile attacks on Iraq, the emotions—in fact, the lives—of people at the other end of U.S. missiles are unimportant.

As consumers of media images, we're offered one insulated kick after another. We easily slip into spectator mode, vicarious and detached.

The euphemisms are wrapped in smug bravado and playground posturing. "A relentless air campaign" is needed. The president should order the Pentagon to "punch out Iraq's lights." Don't spare them—but spare us the grisly details.

[In mid-December 1998, the journalists who had been yearning for a massive military attack on Iraq finally got their wish.]

November 18, 1998

Behind the News Coverage
of Bombing and Bombast

After 1998—a year that culminated with the bombardment of Iraq and the impeachment of President Clinton—we can draw more definite conclusions about key dynamics of America's modern news media. For instance:

- Euphemisms are as common as ever in American reporting of U.S. military actions.

Typically, on the third night of the bombing, CNN's Christiane Amanpour repeatedly told viewers that Baghdad was having a "dramatic" night. When the smoke cleared, she was one of many journalists who spoke of "collateral damage" without mentioning dead Iraqi civilians.

- The U.S. news media, along with the White House and Congress, have no moral authority to condemn terrorism.

During four long nights, while cruise missiles exploded in Baghdad and other populated areas of Iraq, millions of children were among those who lay awake wondering if they would survive till dawn. This terrorism on a grand scale was depicted by major U.S. media as an exercise in righteousness.

- When America's war machine roars and America's media machinery spins, the teeth mesh.

With few exceptions, news reports portrayed the bombing as virtuous, even if a bit unpleasant for some Iraqis.

- After the shooting starts, denunciations of U.S. actions get little ink or air time.

In October 1998, the head of the U.N.'s "oil-for-food" program, Denis Halliday, quit in protest of the sanctions against Iraq. On Dec. 18, while the missiles were flying, he made a statement that wasn't fit for inclusion in media coverage: "The military strikes constitute a futile and short-run irrational action of desperate men."

- In the world according to U.S. mass media, the United Nations is crucial when the U.S. government says it is crucial and irrelevant when the U.S. government says it is irrelevant.

In 1991, when the U.N. Security Council authorized the Gulf War, the American news media elevated the U.N. to the status of Earth's ultimate arbiter. But in 1998, when the United States was unable to get Security Council approval for launching missiles against Iraq, the U.N. was beside the point.

- More than ever, U.S. policy-makers and media elites agree that public debate prior to military action is a risk not worth taking.

In February 1998, when CNN joined with Secretary of State Madeleine Albright and two other top officials to hold a "town hall" meeting in Columbus, Ohio, their weak arguments for attacking Iraq met with effective opposition. At the end of the year, they avoided any such mistake—preferring a mere pantomime of democracy—as mass media and officials went through the motions of open discourse. Likewise, in Congress, substantive debate was somewhere between muted and nonexistent.

- Media outlets mirror White House efforts to portray a U.S. military assault as a conflict with one individual despot.

There was much media enthusiasm for the line that the attacks would "send a message" to Saddam Hussein. But the bombs sent the clear message that the U.S. government views civilian lives as expendable. Rather than impeding the cycles of murderous violence, Washington has insisted on leading the way.

- The news media generally confine themselves to the narrow choices presented by Democratic and Republican leaders.

Benefitting from a carefully crafted media image, Bill Clinton has become a great president for Americans who want the killing sugar-coated and sanitized by liberal piety. Meanwhile, during the first six years of the Clinton administration, harsh sanctions against Iraq have been responsible for the deaths of several hundred thousand people in that country.

- Like the politicians they cover, most American journalists seem to assume that the United States is the center of the universe.

To hear the news media tell it, the recent assault on Iraq was profoundly significant because of possible impacts on partisan power struggles inside the Beltway. In sharp contrast, the people under the bombs were trivial to the punditocracy.

- In medialand, the anguish of Washington's powerful men is much more important than the lives of the human beings they are in the process of killing.

News coverage prompted Americans to shed tears over Clinton's impeachment or Rep. Bob Livingston's resignation—but not over the suffering of Iraqi people.

Now, media outlets are awash in drivel about the crying need for politicians to be nicer to each other.

December 21, 1998

More Important Hoaxes
Get Less Scrutiny

The fall of 1997 began with big news stories about a hoax. Sensational documents—showing that President Kennedy paid hush money to Marilyn Monroe—dazzled a fine journalist and powerful media executives. But they finally realized the documents were fake.

Days after splashy coverage threw cold water on the Monroe-Kennedy papers, another hot item turned into a dud. At first, it had real sizzle: The *New York Times* devoted nearly a quarter of its front page to a new book attributed to an Italian trader who sailed from Europe to southeast China in 1271, four years before Marco Polo's fabled trek.

"A reading of an advance copy suggests that, while it lacks the scope of Marco Polo's epic tale, it has similar historical significance and perhaps greater drama," *Times* foreign correspondent Nicholas Kristof wrote gravely. But eight days later, at the end of September, the publisher (Little, Brown) announced postponement of the book due to serious doubts about its authenticity.

In each instance, the moral of the media story is that even top-notch journalists and sophisticated execs can make mistakes—and that the mass media system works by correcting errors and shining light on the truth.

This may seem reassuring. After all, if media institutions are willing to bite the bullet and admit mistakes, then we don't have much to worry about.

The problem is that mainstream media like to debunk the hoaxes that aren't very important. The relationship between Marilyn Monroe and John Kennedy is not exactly a key issue for our futures. And few modern destinies hinge on whether the public believes that a 13th century Italian merchant made it to China before Marco Polo.

Let's face it: The less weighty a media hoax is, the more likely it will be set straight. And vice versa.

When deceptions cast a huge shadow, they're liable to get scant attention. That's why we're still waiting for the national media to come to terms with hoaxes of recent decades that had profound consequences.

In August 1964, the news media did not hesitate to report falsehoods—supplied by U.S. officials—as absolute facts. What followed, within days, was the congressional Tonkin Gulf resolution—and then a bloody war in Indochina, with a death toll in the millions. But along with other large media outlets, *Newsweek* was never interested in challenging the Tonkin Gulf Hoax, in contrast to the verve of the three-page spread on "The JFK-Marilyn Hoax" in its Oct. 6 [1997] issue.

In late 1990, another big hoax encouraged war. A sobbing Kuwaiti teenager sat before a congressional committee and told of seeing Iraqi invaders pull hundreds of babies from incubators in a Kuwait City hospital.

The tears were shed by the daughter of a Kuwaiti diplomat—and her performance was a scripted lie. But the U.S. media treated the hoax as unvarnished truth, underscoring the need for military action.

On the home front, conventional media wisdom can be so pervasive that years go by with major news organizations busily perpetrating hoaxes rather than exposing them.

A decade ago, news media were filled with claims that the banking industry had to be deregulated in the interests of competition and stability. In 1988, the American Bankers Association gloated that 140 out of 150 newspapers ran editorials in favor of deregulation.

The hoaxers got their way. Deregulation went into effect. The savings-and-loan disaster quickly ensued, with the U.S. Treasury picking up a bailout tab that ballooned to hundreds of billions of dollars.

Today, in Washington and many state capitals, deregulation mania is rampant. Corporate strategists in various industries are euphoric. But—even after consumers and taxpayers get stuck with whopping bills—don't hold your breath for news media to examine the hoaxes that made it all possible.

October 1, 1997

"Virtual History"...
and Virtual Mendacity

This year, thousands of youngsters have gotten involved in "the ultimate multimedia exploration of the American experience."

Virtual history is here—wrapped in a red-white-and-blue package that bears the venerable imprint of *American Heritage* magazine and promises "the only software your kids will ever need to study American history!"

A single CD-ROM disk now provides hours of music, video clips, audio narration and "3D virtual reality walk-throughs." It all comes under a lofty title: "The History of the United States for Young People."

These days, adults are often pleased to see children sitting at computers and learning with a few keystrokes. The scene is so modern... so 21st century!

The kids are learning, all right. But what?

If they're studying, say, the Vietnam War, the computer tells about the escalation of U.S. "air strikes" and then explains: "By the end of the 1960s, bombing raids had become an almost daily occurrence." But the CD-ROM wizardry never gets around to the human suffering caused by those "air strikes" and "bombing raids."

The narrative slant presents Washington's war makers as well-intentioned champions of democratic values. Ironically, kids who use the glitzy history disk to learn about the war in Vietnam are encountering the same distortions that many of their parents and grandparents rejected three decades ago.

Such virtual history may not be any worse than the usual textbook kind. But it can be quite a bit more insidious.

A grotesque visual image—a row of human skulls—appears on the screen when "the South Vietnamese were unable to stop the North Vietnamese advance. In April 1975, commu-nist forces captured Saigon." But the picture of skulls suddenly disappears when other words arrive: "In 1969, President Nixon secretly ordered the bombing of communist bases in Cambodia."

Evidently, in cyberhistory, communist bombs cause ghastly horrors while the effects of American bombs don't merit a blip on the screen. How's that for virtual propaganda?

If this is "the only software your kids will ever need to study American history," we're in big trouble. If "The History of the United States for Young People" is any indication, the current multimedia innovations are opening new vistas for deceiving the next generation.

The more that computers and software become glorified as megabyte beacons of progress for everyday life, the less we hear about GIGO—one of the basic aphorisms that emerged early in the computer age. "Garbage In, Garbage Out."

Vows to put computers in every classroom don't deal with a key question: Are we fixating on the latest gizmos while failing to scrutinize content? The widespread obsessions with technical glitz could amount to perpetual distractions that mesmerize children and adults alike.

The *American Heritage* history disk—which adapts a big-selling schoolbook for eighth-graders—"makes the textbook really come to life," an official who helped produce the CD-ROM told me. But the ultimate target is grown-ups: "It's really for parents to buy for kids."

No one owns America's heritage, of course. But, since 1986, a few rich guys named Forbes have owned *American Heritage*. Steve Forbes—the editor in chief of *Forbes* magazine—is the CEO of the privately held parent company, Forbes Inc.

Forbes ran for president in 1996 and declared: "I want to reduce the [tax] rate further and further and further. We won't get it to zero emissions, you might say, but that wouldn't be a bad goal." That says a lot about what he thinks of government.

Joining with Forbes Inc. to produce "The History of the United States for Young People" is Simon & Schuster, a subsidiary of the media giant Viacom. Clearly, the manufacturing of multimedia history for young people is a very big business.

"Only through history does a nation become completely conscious of itself," wrote the 19th century philosopher Arthur Schopenhauer. "Accordingly, history is to be regarded as the national conscience of the human race."

But what happens when we turn over the national conscience to the high-tech market?

May 21, 1997

Money Scandals:
"Mr. Smith" Goes to Washington

Few politicians are as idealistic as the hero in the classic movie *Mr. Smith Goes to Washington*. But the nation's capital is teeming with journalists who resemble another Mr. Smith—the guy in George Orwell's most famous book.

In *1984*, Winston Smith was employed to dispose of inconvenient bits of history. In real-life newsrooms, the process may be more subtle, but it's often quite Orwellian. Certain awkward facts just don't get into America's media picture.

Case in point: the current uproar over foreign money in American political campaigns.

China is suspected of seeking to influence the outcome of some U.S. congressional races in 1996. That's bad—very bad.

When the United States maneuvered to sway the Russian presidential race in 1996, however, that was good—very good.

"YANKS TO THE RESCUE" blared the cover of *Time* magazine's July 15 [1996] issue, featuring a ten-page spread about a squad of U.S. political pros who "clandestinely participated in guiding [Boris] Yeltsin's campaign."

American resources poured into Russia to help Yeltsin win at the polls. The reaction from journalists? Not even a whimper about the principle of non-intervention in another country's elections.

Actually, the United States makes a habit of such interference around the world.

"U.S. leaders routinely channel millions of tax dollars to political parties in other countries," a Cox News Service article explained. "Private institutes...have used these federal funds to supply equipment, services, training and expert advice on strategy and polling to political parties and other private groups in more than 100 countries."

When the exceptional article appeared in late February [1997], it didn't cause a ripple in the national media pond. "I haven't had any response to the piece," Cox reporter Andrew Mollison told me a couple of weeks later.

Mollison's in-depth story delved into direct U.S. aid to political parties "scattered around the globe and through the alphabet from Albania to Zambia." So, his story was out of sync with the prevailing media script, which typecasts the U.S. government as a victim—not a perpetrator—of anti-democratic plots by foreigners.

The D.C.-based National Endowment for Democracy has rarely faced tough scrutiny from news outlets. Established in 1983, it gets annual funding of $30 million from the federal treasury. The money is used to assist favored political forces overseas. Forty-one of the Duma members now sitting in the Russian parliament, for instance, received campaign aid from one of the endowment's conduits.

Today, the American press—obsessed by Asian money in U.S. politics—would lose its self-righteous tone if it reported some relevant history. A few examples:

ITALY: The CIA provided $10 million for campaigns in Italy's 1972 parliamentary elections and passed along another $6 million for the June 1976 elections.

CHILE: In 1964, eager to defeat socialist Salvador Allende, the CIA got behind the Christian Democratic Party's presidential candidate, Eduardo Frei. "The CIA underwrote more than half the party's total campaign costs," says journalist William Blum. His book *Killing Hope* recounts that "the agency's overall electoral operation reduced the U.S. Treasury by an estimated $20 million—much more per voter than that spent by the Johnson and Goldwater campaigns combined in the same year in the United States."

Six years later, Chile's voters elected Allende president, despite continued U.S. support for his opponents. Allende died in September 1973, when a U.S.-backed coup ushered in seventeen years of bloody dictatorship.

AUSTRALIA: In 1973, when the newly elected Labor Party government charted an independent course in foreign policy, the CIA got very busy—dispensing large amounts of money to conservative parties. Under enormous pressure, the government of Prime Minister Edward Gough Whitlam fell in 1975.

EL SALVADOR: The CIA boosted José Napoleon Duarte to victory in the 1984 presidential contest. Irked because a farther-right candidate lost, Sen. Jesse Helms complained that the CIA had secretly donated $2 million to Duarte's campaign. "In other words, the State Department and the CIA bought the election for Duarte," said Helms.

NICARAGUA: After a decade of the Contras' guerrilla war financed by U.S. taxpayers, the incumbent Sandinistas lost the 1990 election to the pro-U.S. presidential candidate, Violeta Chamorro. Researchers, including former CIA analyst David MacMichael, calculated that U.S. aid to electoral foes of the Sandinistas totaled $26 million between 1984 and 1989 in a country with just 3.5 million people—the equivalent of a foreign infusion into U.S. politics of nearly $2 billion.

Such information belongs in media coverage of the current foreign-money scandal. But America's journalists have dispensed with unpleasant history.

Winston Smith feared for his life. What's their excuse?

March 12, 1997

Part V
Maintaining the Punditocracy

Dream Team for a Media All-Star Game

Renowned baseball players took the field recently for another All-Star game. It's a major-league spectacle that happens with much fanfare every summer. But what would a team of media All-Stars look like?

Here are some possibilities:

STARTING PITCHER: Cokie Roberts

Tossing a classic mix of curveballs and changeups, Roberts can baffle anyone with more than a superficial knowledge of American history. Her delivery, like her wisdom, is utterly conventional.

RELIEVER: Christopher Matthews

The host of the *Hardball* program on a cable-TV network, Matthews now makes frequent use of the spitter when the wind is at his back. Formerly a nominal lefty, he is now proudly ambidextrous.

CLOSER: George Will

This hurler has cultivated an elaborate windup. Yet he can also throw a mean fastball from a stretch position. Will specializes in wide curves that nick the right edge of the plate. Catchers dread handling his knuckler—and sometimes get embarrassed when Will argues that even his wild pitches are strikes. If riled, he resorts to the beanball.

LEADOFF BATTER: Jim Lehrer

His lackadaisical *NewsHour* style belies the fact that Lehrer is adept at the well-placed bunt and beats many throws from across the diamond. Boosted by multi-year endorsement contracts from the agribusiness giant Archer Daniels Midland, he's an excellent corporate-team player.

CLEANUP BATTER: Dan Rather

Off at the crack of a bat, Rather can stretch a cliché into a stand-up triple. He often hits line drives up the middle.

DESIGNATED HITTER: Patrick Buchanan

Known as a "Ty Cobb wannabe" for his flashing spikes and surly manner, this slugger always swings for the fences. Crouched far to the right side of the plate, Buchanan doesn't seem to mind that he rarely connects. Dugout mates say Buchanan complains that batting was much more enjoyable before the days of Roy Campanella.

CENTER FIELDER: Barbara Walters

This consummate pro has decades of experience playing shallow center field. While she defends her turf in the sunny outfield, observers have become heavy-lidded to the point of somnolence.

LEFT FIELDER: Michael Kinsley

Affable and almost erudite, Kinsley has the unfortunate habit of roaming the middle of the outfield for most of each game, thus leaving vast expanses vacant. Some fans swear that he has never come near the left-field line, even to snag a simple pop-up.

RIGHT FIELDER: Rush Limbaugh

Limbaugh, who likes to hug the right-field line, boasts of many putouts in foul territory. However, he is rued by umpires, who find him abusive and prone to hallucinations.

SHORTSTOP: David Gergen

At bat, Gergen is a deft switch hitter. Wearing a mitt, he's a fast man in the pivot—able to pull off a double play with dazzling agility that makes all his maneuvering look easy. Fans marvel that he always seems to land on his feet.

CATCHER: Mike Wallace

This seasoned receiver knows how to call the signals without antagonizing the management.

PINCH HITTER: Katie Couric

Nice and savvy enough to be safe when it counts, Couric makes every *Today* look professional, even when sliding around without purpose.

MANAGER: Bill Gates

If winning is the bottom line and sharing can be understood as market share, then Gates is a great guy to run the team.

BAT BOY: John Journalist

BAT GIRL: Jane Journalist

TEAM MASCOT: Merrill Lynch

TEAM OWNER: Rupert Murdoch

He has a reputation as a foxy mogul with plenty of acumen. But some players grumble that Murdoch's team is weakened by his refusal to allow southpaws on the mound.

STADIUM: TimeWarnerDisneyWestinghouseSonyAT&T-ViacomNewsCorp Park

The media All-Stars wouldn't think of playing the game anywhere else.

July 1, 1998

Some Media Scenes We'd Like to See

Mad Magazine used to dramatize hard-to-imagine events in a section called "Scenes We'd Like to See." In this fanciful feature, TV commercials disclosed the negative aspects of products, and politicians spoke with unflinching candor instead of foggy rhetoric. The imaginary scenarios were as appealing as they were unlikely.

These days, while many professions are undermined by large gaps between routine pretenses and unspoken truths, perhaps none is more full of holes than journalism. So, here are some Media Scenes We'd Like to See:

- SUPERSTAR ANCHORS TURN OVER NEW LEAF
"We've been troubled by the descent of television news into a lucrative swamp of celebrity obsessions and sensationalism," said a joint statement by Tom Brokaw, Peter Jennings and Dan Rather. "Year after year, we continued to be part of the problem. So, we will donate most of our accumulated wealth to a trust fund for independent journalism. And from now on, we'll do what's right, even if that means getting fired by the network brass. There are more important things in life than retaining a multimillion-dollar salary."

- FAMED COLUMNIST REJECTS RACIAL PAST
Commentator George Will, who was a speechwriter for Jesse Helms before becoming a nationally syndicated columnist twenty-five years ago, is now repudiating Sen. Helms and apologizing for their past association. "I was blinded by my own ambition and ideology," said Will. "What's worse, during the past quarter century, I allowed racial biases to influence many of my columns and TV appearances. I deeply regret that I have ranted about low-income black people and their 'pathologies' without questioning my own."

- PANEL OF JOURNALISTS DECRIES COVERAGE OF PALESTINIANS

  An ad hoc committee of reporters, editors and pundits, led by *New York Times* columnist A.M. Rosenthal, lamented the treatment of Palestinian people in America's news media. "I have had a personal awakening on this score," Rosenthal proclaimed. "Now I can see that my fervent support for the state of Israel led me to lose touch with the profound principle that everyone deserves full human rights."

- NEWSPAPER PUBLISHER VOWS REWRITE OF AUTO-BIOGRAPHY

  The longtime owner of the Washington Post Company shocked colleagues and friends by announcing plans to revise her autobiography in the interests of accuracy. Katharine Graham's book *Personal History* won wide acclaim in early 1997—but, according to a new statement released by the author, "most of the reviewers and interviewers were unabashed sycophants." Citing examples of what she called "shamelessly self-serving content," Graham was particularly critical of the book's failure to admit that her close friendships with powerful individuals—such as tycoon Warren Buffett and government officials Robert McNamara and Henry Kissinger—impaired the independence of her employees at the *Washington Post* and *Newsweek*.

- C-SPAN HOST THANKS AUTHOR FOR SETTING RECORD STRAIGHT

  Brian Lamb, the founder of C-SPAN and a prominent host on the cable network, expressed appreciation to author James Ledbetter for exposing a skeleton in Lamb's closet. Published in late 1997, Ledbetter's book—titled *Made Possible By...*—explains that Lamb worked for the Nixon administration and took part in efforts to "shut down public broadcasting." The book reports that Lamb participated in "several meetings to try to get a CPB [Corporation for Public Broadcasting] board that would respond more directly to White House orders." Now,

Lamb says he's glad readers are learning about a period of opportunism that probably helped advance his career.

- HEADS OF NPR AND PBS CONDEMN COMMERCIAL SLIDE

  The presidents of National Public Radio and the Public Broadcasting Service announced that they no longer believe in taking money from big corporations. "We've come to understand that their financial embrace has imposed gradual—and severe—constraints," the leaders of NPR and PBS said. "Calling commercials 'enhanced underwriter credits' doesn't change the fact that you can't have truly public broadcasting when it's dependant on the likes of Archer Daniels Midland, General Electric and Mobil Oil."

Of course, we shouldn't expect to see any such media scenes in the near future. But sometimes, it helps to dream out loud.

January 28, 1998

If Today's Media Covered Past Eras

Have you ever wondered how today's news media would have covered historic events of earlier eras?

If current types of journalism were in place generations ago, the coverage might have gone something like this:

- *CBS Evening News*, Spring 1913

DAN RATHER: "Tensions are high in the nation's capital tonight, hours after a militant march down Pennsylvania Avenue by suffragettes. Police say 3,000 ladies were there. Protest leaders claim twice that number. For some perspective, we turn now to CBS news analyst Laura Ingraham."

LAURA INGRAHAM: "Dan, anyone watching the march had to be concerned about the polarization of America. Gender conflict is on the rise. What's next? Refusal to wear corsets? Brassiere burning? Female lawyers? The latest fashion statements are coming from feminists with an anti-male agenda. It's as though men can't do anything right."

RATHER: "But what about the idea that women should have the right to vote, just like men?"

INGRAHAM: "Sounds like some kind of envy to me, Dan. Those of us who are secure in our womanhood don't make these demands. We may not like the results of the male electorate, but it's the height of elitist arrogance to assume that other voters could do any better."

***

- ABC's *This Week*, March 1933

SAM DONALDSON: "A new president—in a wheelchair no less—entering the White House after a landslide. How's this going to play out? Cokie?"

COKIE ROBERTS: "Sam, it's important that our new president avoid doing anything rash. Let's remember, he wisely campaigned on a moderate platform. Now, as usual, some Democrats want to push him to the left. It would be political suicide."

GEORGE WILL: "The leveling impulse has always been a hazard to democracy, as Alexis de Tocqueville pointed out a century ago. He warned that Americans were overly enamored with equality, which can only lead to the tyranny of the mob. Right now, I fear for this republic."

DONALDSON: "George, surely you're not saying Franklin Roosevelt is dangerous. I mean —"

WILL: "Time will tell. There's talk of a federal social-security program. And unemployment insurance. The kind of welfare-state mentality that undermines family values and frays the moral fabric of the free-enterprise system."

ROBERTS: "But I'm convinced cooler heads will prevail. That's the word on Capitol Hill."

***

- Headlines, July 1946

PEOPLE MAGAZINE: "Bob Oppenheimer, the Sexy Brain Behind the Bomb Tests"

WALL STREET JOURNAL: "Bikini A-Bomb Blasts Encourage Investors"

USA TODAY: "We're Happy About Atomic Weapons!"

***

- ABC's *20/20*, September 1957

HUGH DOWNS: "It's not so easy being a governor these days. Is it, Barbara?"

BARBARA WALTERS: "Certainly not if your name is Orval Faubus. I visited him yesterday at the governor's mansion in Little Rock. He was kind and charming. But his life has been quite stressful with all the well-publicized controversy about integration at Central High School. Next: a look inside the private life of the governor of Arkansas, a gentle man in a difficult time."

***

• *The McLaughlin Group*, April 1963

FRED BARNES: "This kind of lawlessness can't be tolerated. It's outrageous."

MORTON KONDRACKE: "A big publicity stunt, that's what we're seeing. Some of my gullible colleagues in the press corps are falling for this smear campaign against the city of Birmingham, the state of Alabama and the United States of America. These demonstrations give comfort to our country's enemies."

PATRICK BUCHANAN: "The protesters say they want 'civil rights.' What a laugh. They want special rights. If the media would ignore these troublemakers, we'd have some racial tranquility in America. The police measures have been entirely justified."

JACK GERMOND: "Gosh, I can't agree with that. Maybe the fire hoses are necessary. But using attack dogs on those young demonstrators seems too extreme."

JOHN McLAUGHLIN: "Jack, is that the bleating sound of a bleeding-heart liberal?"

KONDRACKE: "Ha ha."

BARNES: "Ha ha."

July 16, 1997

Truth or Consequences
for News Media

We like to think that journalists will pay a heavy price if they tell lies or promote deception. But it ain't necessarily so.

Consider the case of former *Newsweek* writer Joe Klein.

Throughout the first half of 1996, Klein denied that he was "Anonymous"—the author of the hot new political novel *Primary Colors*. Klein's denials were frequent and vehement. But in mid-1996, the world learned that he'd been lying the whole time.

A year later, Klein was riding high as Washington correspondent for the prestigious *New Yorker* magazine.

Klein built his career largely by accusing inner-city blacks of "dependency" and "pathology." He often stereotyped them as dishonest. In retrospect—considering his awesome display of dishonesty—the ironies abound.

A few days ago, I asked Klein whether those ironies had caused him to reassess the superior tone of his numerous articles that looked down on the moral standards of poor African Americans. He replied: "Are you out of your mind?"

Klein wasn't the only *Newsweek* journalist implicated in the Anonymous subterfuge. The editor of the magazine, Maynard Parker, knew that Klein was the author of *Primary Colors* all along—and stayed silent. In fact, Parker allowed his magazine to print misleading speculation about the author's identity.

When his complicity came to light, Parker was unrepentant. He urged critics to "get a life."

Today, Maynard Parker is still the editor of *Newsweek*. And though Joe Klein took a great deal of flak from colleagues, he told me that his exit from the magazine in November 1996 was purely voluntary: "I quit." Without any delay, Klein was comfortably ensconced at *The New Yorker*, covering politics.

From the outset of his Anonymous gambit (calculated to hike book sales), Klein might have guessed that he wasn't risking much. For comfort, he may have thought of columnist George Will.

Will is "perhaps the most powerful journalist in America," according to the *Wall Street Journal*. But back in October 1980, Will skated over some very thin ice when he went on ABC's *Nightline* to praise Ronald Reagan's "thoroughbred performance" in a crucial debate with incumbent President Jimmy Carter.

There was something that Will didn't mention. He had helped coach Reagan for that debate—and had read Carter's briefing materials stolen from the White House.

Will's devious role remained a secret for years. When it finally surfaced, other journalists politely chided him and dropped the subject. Instead of slumping, Will's career gained star quality.

"What brought him to outer space was exactly the thing many thought would bring him down: coaching Reagan," observed Jeff Greenfield of ABC News. "To the skill and style he'd always had, it added the insider magic."

Perhaps few journalists have outdone Klein and Will for brazen duplicity. But many of America's eminent news reporters make a habit of presenting deceptive claims from government sources as credible.

Predictably, a lot of Washington-based journalists with long experience in misleading the public have denounced the *San Jose Mercury News* series that linked the CIA-backed Nicaraguan Contras with the spread of crack cocaine in the United States during the early 1980s.

In recent weeks—ever since the top editor at the *Mercury News*, Jerry Ceppos, wrote a column retreating from some aspects of the series—we've heard plenty of media pieties about how the series failed to include more than one interpretation of facts. Yet news pages and broadcasts often contain just one limited interpretation—drawn from official sources.

Late last month [May 1997], an article by veteran journalist Daniel Schorr in the *Christian Science Monitor* put the uproar in perspective. Usually no maverick, Schorr stepped out of the media herd this time, writing that "big newspapers lost sight of the fact that Ceppos had said the series was right on many important points."

Schorr went against the prevalent trashing of a courageous, truth-seeking journalist: "Odd man out in this controversy is investigative reporter Gary Webb, the hard-working author of the series. He was left to twist in the wind while the press glorified his editor for having some second thoughts about the explosive articles."

Meanwhile, Joe Klein isn't twisting in any wind. Neither is George Will. And neither are the journalists who never tell lies—but pass them along from official sources and avoid the risks of telling hard truths.

June 4, 1997

Part VI
Deferring to Elites

Elite Preoccupations Leave
Other Concerns in Shadows

Two recent events—the launch of a magazine about news media and the release of a survey about journalists' opinions—illustrate the wide gap between the preoccupations of elite media professionals and the economic outlooks of most Americans.

After lots of advance publicity, the premiere [August 1998] issue of *Brill's Content* is hot off the press. The magazine calls itself "the Independent Voice of the Information Age" and pledges to scrutinize news coverage without fear or favor. But so far, the match-up seems to be along the lines of "Establishment vs. Establishment."

Exactly who owns this "independent voice"? Along with Steven Brill, the other investors behind the magazine are media magnate Barry Diller, real estate tycoon Howard Milstein and financier Lester Pollack.

What is the size of their investments? Other than declaring that Brill is the "majority owner," spokespeople for *Brill's Content* remain tight-lipped. The magazine's editorial director, Michael Kramer, told me: "We don't disclose the percentages."

Will the magazine probe the media empire of co-owner Diller? Now the head of USA Networks Inc., he is known as the pioneer of home shopping channels. Today, Diller's network airs a lot of TV programs, including *The Jerry Springer Show*.

Inadvertently, *Brill's Content* has already dramatized a key point: Ownership affects media content.

For the magazine's first issue, editors commissioned Tom Tomorrow to provide a full-page cartoon. But later on, Tomorrow received an unexpected call from Executive Editor Amy Bernstein. "Steve [Brill] doesn't agree with it, and we're just not going to run it," the cartoonist recalls her saying. When I phoned Bernstein, she confirmed: "Steve just didn't like it."

Ironically, the rejected cartoon had addressed just such dynamics. It said: "Most journalists WILL acknowledge—at least, after a drink or two—that the news outlets they work for DO tend to be biased—in favor of THEIR OWNER'S INTERESTS, that is."

Now, we can thank the main owner of *Brill's Content* for demonstrating the truth he found unfit to print: Owners can tilt the content of the media outlets they own.

There is some solid journalism in *Brill's Content*, such as the "Pressgate" cover story that spells out how "the press seems to have become an enabler" of Independent Counsel Kenneth Starr's "abuse of power." But according to articles in this issue of the magazine, the most aggrieved victims of unfair media coverage are elites: President Clinton, Sen. Robert Byrd, the company that makes the Audi 5000 luxury sedan.

Unfortunately, *Brill's Content* mirrors the overall preoccupations of mainstream media: Are particular politicians getting a fair shake? Are corporations being mistreated? Such fixations leave little room for other concerns—such as economic inequities.

When the interests of owners find resonance with the views of most journalists, the confluence of biases can be especially powerful. And that's where a new survey of the Washington press corps comes in. The media watch group FAIR has just released the results of the survey, which sheds new light on the myth of the "liberal media."

Previous FAIR studies have debunked much of the myth by documenting the heavy reliance on centrist, conservative and corporate news sources by mainstream media programs such as ABC's *Nightline*, the PBS *NewsHour* and NPR's weekday *All Things Considered* and *Morning Edition*.

But during the past few years, another part of the "liberal media" fable has been widely propagated—the notion that most reporters are secret leftists.

The new data from FAIR (a group that I'm associated with) provide some clarity. In a survey conducted by sociologist David Croteau of Virginia Commonwealth University,

Washington journalists expressed views on economic issues that were more conservative—not more "liberal"—than those of the general public.

The responses from 141 journalists indicate that the Washington press corps is to the right of most Americans on various economic issues, including taxation of the wealthy, Social Security and health care. (Details of the survey results are available at www.fair.org.)

Here's an example from the FAIR survey: Do a few large companies have "too much power"? Journalists—answering yes 57 percent of the time—were much more evenly divided than the public. National opinion samples have consistently found Americans to be strongly affirmative on the question, with 77 percent responding yes in one poll.

Evidence keeps piling up: The priorities and preoccupations of elite journalists are far afield from the economic concerns of most Americans.

June 17, 1998

Press Flails as Lawmakers
Make Mess of House

Bad Congress! Bad Congress!

Lawmakers on Capitol Hill have gotten quite a media scolding lately. You'd think they were dogs that refused to be "Housebroken." From coast to coast, the angry sound of rolled-up newspapers was unmistakable.

The *New York Times* held its nose in disgust all the way through an editorial that thrashed "vengeful" Democrats in the House of Representatives for failing to grant the president fast-track power over trade agreements [in November 1997]. The newspaper concluded that "narrow political interest has carried the day."

Meanwhile, a *Washington Post* editorial was fuming that Congress "caved in to the special pleaders." The editorial made an odd claim: "Trade liberalization benefits most people, but it also invariably hurts a few... In the political process, the losers and potential losers naturally lobby vociferously; the winners, a larger but more diffuse group, don't."

The *Post* didn't mention that trade-deal "winners" had been able to lobby vociferously in its own pages. During the six months leading up to fast track's demise in the House, the *Post*'s op-ed page ran twelve articles in favor of fast track—and just four against it.

When Congress declined to give fast track a green light, many pundits with big megaphones expressed anger. None were more contemptuous than *Washington Post* columnist James Glassman, who described the House of Representatives as "the Washington chapter of the Flat Earth Society." He proclaimed: "It's hard to find a respectable economist who opposes free trade, the value of which is glaringly obvious."

As a fellow at the American Enterprise Institute, one of the nation's most influential think tanks, Glassman doesn't let the readers of his widely syndicated column know who is paying the piper for his tunes. But a report by Public Citizen documented that between 1992 and 1995, the Institute received more than $1.7 million from pharmaceutical, medical device, biotechnology and tobacco firms and their foundations—only some of the donors eager for "free trade" pacts that curb government regulation.

Glassman—who described Democrats in Congress as "the disingenuous stewards of unions that are desperately trying to maintain their cartels"—was among numerous commentators who blasted organized labor for going toe-to-toe with big business on the fast-track issue.

A *Los Angeles Times* opinion piece that appeared Nov. 12 [1997] was typical: Political scientist Ross K. Baker denounced "labor's scare tactics" and contended that "congressional Democrats have consented to be bound, trussed and gagged by America's fading labor movement."

In the wake of fast track's failure to get through the House, a *Wall Street Journal* editorial mournfully charged that AFL-CIO President John Sweeney had "busted up a Democratic president's attempt to maintain American trade leadership in the emerging global economy."

A lot of news and commentary echoed the sentiments of Commerce Secretary William Daley, who depicted citizens living outside the Beltway as ill-informed dummies: "Even though we all know the benefits of globalization, obviously the people out there don't know it."

But, at a Boston-based group called United for a Fair Economy, researcher Chuck Collins observes that "the American people are not isolationist or stupid about the ups and downs of free trade." He points out: "Americans are suspicious of international trade policies that are written entirely to serve the interests of large multinational corporations."

When those interests won a big victory with passage of NAFTA in 1993, news coverage tended to portray the win as a triumph for pro-trade rationality. But the big victory over fast-track legislation—won by labor, environmentalists and human rights activists—was widely reported as a triumph for narrow special interests.

Lori Wallach, director of Public Citizen's Global Trade Watch, has an assessment that's very different from the usual fast-track post mortems in the news media. "Despite the incredible pressure of the president and the Cabinet, despite the offers of outrageous pork-barrel deals, despite the intense lobbying by most of the Fortune 500," she says, "Congress was able to represent the interests of their constituents."

Whether the country's powerful media outlets like it or not, disobedient voices have transformed the national debate.

November 12, 1997

Making Sense of
Wall Street's Roller Coaster

When Wall Street turns into a roller coaster, it's big news. And that's appropriate. No one can question the huge quantity of coverage that the stock market has gotten lately. But the quality is another matter.

At first, a market plunge is apt to resemble a spectator sport—far more exciting and consequential than the World Series and the Super Bowl put together. News accounts are filled with dramatic numbers and breathless profiles of key players. We see photos and footage of crowds—often panicky traders soaked with sweat in a stock-exchange pit.

Within hours, the emphasis shifts to reassurance. When the last week of October [1997] began with a 554-point drop of the Dow Jones Industrial Average, a lot of editorials quickly offered soothing messages. Yet many readers must have scratched their heads and wished for a decoder.

One observer who's notably adept at cracking the code of media econospeak is Doug Henwood, author of a new book titled *Wall Street: How It Works and For Whom*. He's not a conventional pundit. Instead of repeating the standard euphemisms, he debunks them.

So, I asked Henwood to help interpret the Oct. 28 *New York Times* editorial headlined "The Plunging Dow."

- "There is reason to believe that a resilient economy and Federal Reserve intervention can prevent avalanche selling on Wall Street from burying jobs and income on Main Street," the editorial declared.

The clear message was "Don't worry, don't sell, don't panic. Everything's going to be all right."

But the editorial had a less obvious subtext. Henwood summarized it this way: "Government policy-makers have shredded the safety net for the penniless and the sick, but it's still there for financiers." The era of dependency might be over for welfare recipients but not for investors.

- "Stock crashes create problems for banks, securities firms and mutual funds that are hit by a rush of investors redeeming shares and demanding cash," the *Times* editorialized. "But the Fed has the luxury of working with a banking system that is flush with reserves and the leeway to pump money into an economy that is almost inflation-free."

Henwood's translation of that passage: "There's good inflation, which is rising stock prices. And there's bad inflation, which is rising wages."

In fact, the day after the big Oct. 27 plunge, the stock market was heartened by release of a new report on the Employment Cost Index, which showed that worker pay has barely risen in the United States. Not exactly good news on Main Street—but great news on Wall Street, where wages for you and me are viewed as onerous "costs."

- "The economy's vital signs are strong, which reflects many years of solid monetary and fiscal policies that should now serve Americans well," the *Times* editorial concluded.

The phrase "solid monetary and fiscal policies" referred to tight money and federal budget balancing—measures that have long been showered with media praise. But, according to Henwood, "there's no evidence that they serve the bottom three-quarters [of the public] well in terms of income distribution." He added: "The top 5 percent of the population has captured almost all of the economic growth of the past two decades."

While Wall Streeters hung on during a wild-ride week, *Time* magazine was telling millions of readers: "We live in an unusual period of low inflation, achieved in a big way by companies cutting costs to the bone to keep prices down." However, back in the real world, firms aren't cutting costs "to keep prices down"— they're doing it to boost profit margins as high as possible.

"Cutting costs" wouldn't sound so laudable if the details were mentioned—such as using more temporary labor, slashing benefits, suppressing unions, closing plants and relocating. As Henwood points out, companies "have been getting pressure, from their shareholders and Wall Street, to increase profits by cutting costs—squeezing labor, moving production abroad, the usual array of corporate austerity policies."

Doug Henwood is not invited onto the TV networks to discuss economic issues. Overall, there's little room in the mass media for someone with his outlook—whether Wall Street is a roller coaster or a smooth ride.

October 29, 1997

Media Encouraged
Clinton's Embrace of Fatcats

After years of urging Bill Clinton to be a "New Democrat"and lie down with corporate dogs, the press is now marveling that his presidency is infested with scandalous fleas.

Conventional media wisdom has always been that President Clinton should be "moderate" and "centrist"—catering to the economic establishment. Over the years, Clinton has drawn profuse media praise for doing just that.

Back in early 1993, top White House aides defended Clinton's first budget by boasting of its "pro-business slant." Since then, the dominant news media have demanded—and gotten—a president striving to satisfy the centers of financial power.

A natural outcome of corporate-friendly politics is that wealthy donors line up to buy influence. Many journalists pushed the White House to fix big-money omelets and now are wailing about all the ethical eggs that got cracked.

Of course Clinton is going to seek large contributions from people who appreciate his eagerness to make them richer. What's he supposed to do—ask for dollar bills from the working-class Americans he has betrayed?

Midway through his first term, Clinton set about raising millions to ward off any challenge to renomination in the Democratic primaries. When the strategy worked, media outlets widely applauded Clinton's maneuver as smart politics that helped to subdue his party's left wing.

Clinton's hardball zeal at playing the money game attracted many fans in the Washington press corps. And leading pundits cheered when Clinton repeatedly portrayed the corporate agenda—NAFTA, "free trade" and so forth—as key to America's role in the world.

For several years, news media have lauded Clinton for putting the interests of U.S.-based corporations at the forefront of foreign policy. The president won accolades for his global vision. Many journalists voiced enthusiasm as the Commerce Department became immersed in high-rolling projects overseas.

Commerce Secretary William Daley—like his predecessors Mickey Kantor and the late Ron Brown—rose to prominence by matching big donors with political doers. When Daley got Clinton's nod in December 1996, most of the press responded warmly. The *Washington Post*'s influential commentator David Broder quickly told CNN viewers that the Daley appointment was "terrific."

Time magazine seemed positively lighthearted when it described the incoming economic team for Clinton's second term as a "firm"—"a bunch of investment bankers and lawyers, friendly to the stock market." The upbeat article reported that Robert Rubin "is thoroughly entrenched as treasury secretary and a kind of managing partner." One banking analyst explained that the new Clinton appointees "are exactly what Wall Street wants."

The blatant transfer of government policy-making to elite financiers has become so routine that past arrogance hardly seems remarkable now. In early 1993, Rubin became the president's "chief economic adviser" after receiving $17 million for his services as co-chair of Goldman, Sachs and Company the previous year. As he was moving from Wall Street to Pennsylvania Avenue, Rubin sent a matter-of-fact note to his corporate clients, saying: "I look forward to continuing to work with you in my new capacity."

Clinton's shameless privatization of federal economic decisions did not set off warning bells in the news media. On the contrary, year after year, it enhanced the president's glowing credentials as a New Democrat—unburdened by old-fashioned allegiances to labor and the poor.

These days, outrage is all the rage as Clinton's sleazier fund-raising gambits come to light. But the media outcry is taking place largely because he was so brazen about trading White House access for big bucks.

At the White House in late February [1997], the president proclaimed: "They were my friends and I was proud to have them here. I did not have any strangers here." In effect, Clinton was saying: *Any friend of the corporate system can be a friend of mine.*

Overall, the news media have welcomed those affinities in the past. The current uproar is due to the president's clumsy implementation.

The same journalists who have long admired Clinton's savvy, corporate-hugging centrism are now shaking their heads. They don't really fault Clinton for prostituting his presidency to corporate interests. The scandal is that he went about it in such a tacky way.

February 26, 1997

A Hollow Core at the "Vital Center"

Despite the scandalmania of 1998, Bill Clinton now appears to be rather entrenched in the White House. A big reason is that he has been very careful to stay near the middle of America's political spectrum.

The "vital center"—a phrase that was dormant for several decades—became a mantra for Clinton's second term. On Dec. 11, 1996, in his first major policy speech after winning re-election, the president vowed to "forge a coalition of the center." And he called for "a vital American center where there is cooperation across lines of party and philosophy."

Appropriately, Clinton delivered the speech to a forum hosted by the Democratic Leadership Council—a group that has enjoyed plenty of favorable media coverage since he and Al Gore helped to found it in 1985.

From the outset, while loudly claiming to speak for America's middle class, the DLC owed its prominence to generous financial support from decidedly upper-class patrons: Arco, Dow Chemical, Georgia Pacific, Martin Marietta, the Petroleum Institute and other denizens of corporate America.

As a matter of routine, well-heeled lobbyists flocked to DLC functions. "There's no question you can define 'special interest' as our sponsors," the DLC's president, Al From, acknowledged with rare candor. In March 1989, when From's group held its annual conference, nearly 100 lobbyists subsidized the event by paying between $2,500 and $25,000 each. A year later, in the spring of 1990, Clinton began his stint as chair of the DLC.

Writing in the September/October 1998 issue of *The New Democrat*, the DLC's magazine, From credited his organization with laying the groundwork for "Third Way politics" that have swept the United States as well as much of Europe and Latin America. "The Third Way's roots are firmly planted in our New Democrat movement," he declared. "Indeed, the Democratic Leadership Council has a rightful claim to paternity."

What does all this talk about the "vital center" and the "Third Way" really mean?

Amid a geyser of misty rhetoric (for instance, "the Third Way is the worldwide brand name for progressive politics for the Information Age"), Al From supplies a basic clue. "Third Way governments," he explains, "create opportunities, rather than guarantee outcomes." Such buzzwords are common among DLC hotshots and their powerful allies inside the Democratic Party.

Mark Penn, a top DLC pollster and strategist, rejoices that "the Democratic Party is moving into the vital center of American politics and away from the political left." He contends that "the views of voters who identify themselves as Democrats today are converging with those of the American electorate as a whole in the vital center of American politics." And, he asserts, "Democratic success lies in advocating a government that provides opportunity, not guarantees."

Emphasis on opportunity for all Americans has been central to the jargon of the Clinton presidency. And the news media have loved it.

But is "opportunity" sufficient? Even if each person faced the same odds (a far cry from social realities), would we praise a lottery for providing everyone with an "opportunity" to win? What about the losers?

Should we idealize a society for providing most people with health care and a roof over their heads—even if millions of people lack access to medical treatment and many individuals are homeless?

Advocates for the vital center and the Third Way are likely to shrug. After all, it's not appropriate to "guarantee outcomes."

Huge gaps between rich and poor? Don't bother us about "outcomes." A lot of poverty in our midst? Well, everybody has an opportunity to succeed. Scant regulatory curbs on large corporations? Hey, the era of big government is over.

Centrist approaches are usually based on power, not equity or justice. Consider some recent words from the author of the 1949 book titled *The Vital Center*.

Last spring, in an article for *Society* magazine, Arthur Schlesinger Jr. wrote that the "vital center" phrase in his famous book "refers to the contest between democracy and totalitarianism, not to contests within democracy between liberalism and conservatism, not at all to the so-called 'middle of the road' preferred by cautious politicians of our own time."

Schlesinger added: "The middle of the road is definitely not the vital center—it is the dead center."

But to most politicians and journalists, the center of power and wealth is the vital center, no matter how hollow it may be for the less fortunate.

October 14, 1998

Part VII
Dancing to Money Tunes

Worshipping the New Media Gods

The cover of *Time* magazine showed Apple co-founder Steve Jobs on bended knee, holding a cell phone and telling the head man at Microsoft: "Bill, thank you. The world's a better place."

Huh?

The sudden Microsoft-Apple alliance was also on the *Newsweek* cover, which displayed a lively argument. "Bill Gates is good for Apple," said one senior editor. "No, he isn't," said another.

A fierce debate—within very narrow bounds.

And so it goes. The titans of the computer industry stride the media heavens. Bill Gates is our modern-day Zeus. Other gods are overwhelmed by his amazing powers. What a story!

Meanwhile, back on the ground, mortals can only imagine what it's like to move corporate mountains and build digital highways with the flick of a pen. We're encouraged to look up with awe at the colossal deal makers.

They're creating the software in our drives and the images on our screens—and, increasingly, the dreams in our heads. They are the Providers. We are the consumers.

The reverence in the air leaves an acrid smell. We may resent the Lord of Microsoft and the lesser gods, but the media culture of worship seems almost overpowering. An ultramodern theology now glorifies the quest for vast wealth and technological power.

A decade ago, the advertising critic Leslie Savan noted the emergence of what she called "secular fiscalism." Television commercials were starting to tout the accumulation of capital "as an expression of inner spiritual growth."

In 1986, Savan described a new MasterCard slogan—"Master the Possibilities"—as "apparently est-inspired." She added that a Merrill Lynch ad campaign, "Your World Should

Know No Boundaries," was linking investment with traditional religious images of "God's country."

By the early 1990s, such commercials were common. Savan dubbed them "spiritual ads" and observed that they "help us to simultaneously see our shallow, materialistic ways *and* exorcise them: We can consume the evil of excess by making every purchase into a prayer."

And yet, Savan pointed out, those ads "clang with the contradiction between the abundant material life that commercial culture pushes and the more mystical injunction to shed that abundance in order to focus on what really matters." The contradiction "is readily resolved by the ads' *passive* spirituality—be impressed by killer sunsets, feel awe from celestial music—which works right into a consumer kind of spirituality."

During the first years after World War II, sociologist C. Wright Mills saw the trend coming. He warned that money-driven fixations among elites were having enormous effects on the entire society—causing people to shape themselves to fit the "higher immorality" of corporate America and "the social premiums that prevail."

The process was insidious and did not provoke a sense of public crisis, Mills wrote in his 1956 book *The Power Elite*. He called attention to "a creeping indifference and a silent hollowing out." And he commented: "Money is the one unambiguous criterion of success, and such success is still the sovereign American value… It is not only that men want money; it is that their very standards are pecuniary."

When such standards hold sway, even fame and fortune are not enough. The dominant concept is always "more."

Maybe you've seen the new TV spot featuring one of the most acclaimed novelists alive, Kurt Vonnegut, who appears in a commercial for Discover Card. He talks about buying his own books at a store: "I presume I got a royalty as well as the bonus from Discover Card."

Must all knees bend in the direction of Dollar Almighty? Of course not. Despite the intense pressures, plenty of resistance continues. But deeper values must withstand the assaults from the monetary worship that proliferates in the mass media every day.

August 13, 1997

Internet Shopping Network:
The Malling of Cyberspace

Are you ready for the Internet Shopping Network?

Ready or not, here it comes. The guy who pioneered home shopping channels on television, Barry Diller, is now blazing trails into cyberspace.

Despite the stock market's current jitters about such ventures, Diller plans to go forward in 1999 with an initial public offering for the Internet Shopping Network. It's part of his effort to become "electronic-commerce czar," according to the *Wall Street Journal*—which reports that Diller "is once again demonstrating his ability to position himself at the cusp of the business world's next big thing."

Strip-malling the Internet is quite a concept.

Not long ago, we kept hearing about "the information superhighway." But these days, that sounds almost quaint. Images linking the vast Internet to exploration and discovery now take a back seat to media preoccupations with the wonders of marketing and buying, cyber-style.

The emergence of the Internet Shopping Network is a symbol of how coolly calculating heads are prevailing over gushy platitudes about democratic discourse in cyberspace.

More than ever, a visit to the opening screens of America Online or CompuServe indicates just how tightly the biggest online services are interwoven with the nation's largest TV networks, weekly magazines, daily papers, wire services and the like. The medium of the Internet is new, but its main "content providers" are mostly providing the same old content.

Meanwhile, as traditional media outlets supply endless hype for some aspects of the World Wide Web, the touted heroes are often entrepreneurs who combine high-tech computer advances with shrewd marketing strategies. Implicit in such coverage is the assumption that colonizing the New World of cyberspace—with corporate enthusiasm that echoes notions of Manifest Destiny—is logical, creative and laudable.

There is a case to be made for allowing commercial interests to dominate the Internet. It's similar to cases that were made for commercializing other technologies at pivotal stages of media development—radio in the early 1930s, broadcast television at mid-century and cable TV in the 1970s.

At all those historic junctures, lofty rhetoric has been expended to justify the prerogatives of capital. But in each instance, the underlying quest can be summed up in two words: maximize profits.

Spin the radio dial, or click through the channels of a TV set, and you may—or may not—appreciate what reliance on the "free market" has produced. Overall, the airwaves and cable byways have been ravaged by unflagging zeal to shoot the bottom line through the roof.

The Internet is apt to seem very different. Unlimited and decentralized, it's far more participatory than radio and television. Cyberspace has much lower barriers for people with something to say.

Freedom of speech is one thing, however, and freedom to be widely heard is another. You can put up a website. But if you want to reach a mass audience, you'll need either a lot of money or promotional backing from some entity with a lot of money. The exceptions are rare counterpoints to the dominant rule.

As an emerging lord of cyberspace, Barry Diller is a perfect example of grim synergy. He now runs USA Networks Inc., which produces *The Jerry Springer Show* as part of its array of TV output. Diller has the resources to launch his Internet Shopping Network into the media heavens.

"Television programming and direct selling are related," Diller explains, "and our bet is that they will become more related."

Conveniently, media magnates tend to have plenty of influential pals and business partners. For instance, Diller doesn't worry about any tough-minded scrutiny of the Internet Shopping Network by the country's largest-circulation magazine of media criticism, *Brill's Content*. Diller is one of the magazine's four owners.

None of this means that we should be discouraged from doing all we can to use the Internet for independent purposes. Many individuals and groups around the world are doing just that. But let's get the cyber-stars out of our eyes.

Technologies don't create vibrant public debate or democratize societies. People do—or at least they can try.

October 28, 1998

After El Niño Blows Over, "El Bunko" Will Remain

As winter gets underway, much of the nation is bracing for turbulent weather. Recent news stories have heralded the ominous arrival of El Niño. But what about "El Bunko"?

They're quite different: El Niño is an occasional climate shift that comes from nature. El Bunko is a perennial media pattern that comes from human activity.

If we see El Niño approaching, we're likely to batten down the hatches and take a variety of precautions. But El Bunko is apt to be welcomed as an informative flood of news.

People are concerned that El Niño might engulf their homes with storm water—but they often swallow the deluge provided by El Bunko.

El Niño is a mass of unusually warm ocean water, causing upheaval in weather patterns. El Bunko is the mass media's usual hot air, causing perceptual distortions.

While the damage done by El Niño can be estimated, the harm that results from the El Bunko effect is so extensive as to be incalculable. No insurance company in the world could write a policy to cover what it's costing us.

El Bunko is a system of manipulation, serving movers and shakers around the globe. A lot of their maneuvering is out in the open—though furtive meetings are certainly useful to facilitate the process.

Most of all, El Bunko is a non-stop barrage of words and images, obscuring rather than clarifying.

When prestigious journalists tell us that "the economy" is doing great—without reference to the realities of widespread poverty—El Bunko is gathering steam.

When wealthy elites develop new plans for turning Robin Hood upside down by taking resources from the poor and middle class in many lands, you'll hear the tempests of El Bunko howling about the need for more "market reform."

117

When U.S. government officials proclaim that Asian nations must "drop barriers to foreign investment"—while media pundits cheer—El Bunko's wind machines are in high gear.

When the mightiest economic institution on the planet offers Third World countries huge lines of credit—under strict conditions, of course—you'll hear the El Bunko chorus singing the praises of the global loan shark known as the International Monetary Fund.

When news reports barely mention that those IMF conditions require scores of governments to slash programs for such human needs as nutrition, health care and education, El Bunko is packing a ferocious punch. Later, the death toll goes uncounted.

And when big-money titans stride across borders, flattening barriers to their dominance, you can count on El Bunko to depict resistance as old-fashioned "protectionism."

After a rough winter, El Niño will blow over. But behind El Bunko is a high-pressure system of corporate power that promises to gain strength for a very long time.

At the end of the 19th century, Ambrose Bierce defined the corporation as "an ingenious device for obtaining individual profit without individual responsibility." The definition still holds. But near the end of this century, the profits—and grim consequences—of this ingenious device are beyond anything the author of *The Devil's Dictionary* could have imagined.

In their recent book, *The Global Media: The New Missionaries of Corporate Capitalism*, Edward S. Herman and Robert W. McChesney predict that current trends will continue "for the short and medium term."

But despite the reasons for gloom, Herman and McChesney see more than a bleak horizon: "What is done now may significantly affect what is possible later. The system may be far more vulnerable and subject to change than appears to be the case at present... If it is to change, and in a positive way, it is important that people who are dissatisfied with the status quo should not be overcome and rendered truly powerless by a sense of hopelessness and cynicism."

Perhaps the grandest achievement of the El Bunko effect is to make the existing political climate seem natural. We're supposed to believe that pillaging the planet is part of an inevitable progression. But it isn't.

El Niño is nature. El Bunko is something else.

December 10, 1997

The Media Habits of
Dr. Jekyll and Mr. Hype

While tracking the Monica Lewinsky scandal, many prominent journalists have resembled tigers, eager to pounce on President Clinton. With some other issues, in sharp contrast, they behave more like lapdogs.

When reporting on the Lewinsky matter, the national press corps has ripped into Clinton's statements to expose evasions and inconsistencies. But when it comes to reporting on President Clinton's economic priorities, the same journalists usually echo his assertions without question.

Everyone is aware that media outlets are routinely focusing on salacious news. And when pundits go through the ritual of voicing their disapproval, they're apt to blame entertainment mania. "We now know that ideology has nothing to do with which scandals get major media attention," *New York Times* columnist Frank Rich proclaimed in late February [1998]. "The only criterion that really matters is, is it entertaining enough?"

That's an easy diagnosis for what ails the news media. Too easy.

Sure, crass commercialism has pushed the mainstream media into an obsession with titillating stories about celebrities. But let's get a grip. Do we really hunger for bigger helpings of standard reportage—the kind, say, that "informed" the public about the Gulf of Tonkin incident in 1964 or the Central American wars of the 1980s?

To hear the mass media's favorite critics tell it, the press is suffering from some kind of professional schizophrenia—a malady of Dr. Jekyll and Mr. Hype. According to this fantasy, the good doctors of journalism have drugged themselves with tawdry sensationalism. If only they would return to their prior condition of virtue!

But more news coverage is no better than less if distortion is still routine, with reporters relying on official sources in

Washington and corporate sources on Wall Street to set the tone and provide the slant. Simply bemoaning the shrinkage of traditional news is like griping that a restaurant with a long record of serving rancid food has cut back on the size of the portions.

Overall, Americans receive most of their news in skewed patterns. For one thing, the glorification of profit above all other values is itself an ideology—though by now it's so widespread that it blends into the media scenery, appearing to be part of the natural world. Meanwhile, enormous amounts of media resources go into uncovering and dramatizing certain information, while a pittance is devoted to bringing other realities to light.

The themes that hold sway in print and on the airwaves generally reflect the ideologies of media owners, advertisers and underwriters. Big-money pressures and constraints on media content loom large because they take institutional form. In the long run, those who pay the piper don't finance too many threatening tunes—and most of what remains is music to big corporate ears.

But, once in a while, some very discordant notes still get through. In a Feb. 25 [1998] commentary on National Public Radio's *Morning Edition*, political analyst Kevin Phillips offered the kind of blunt assessment rarely heard in mass media.

Reviewing economic data of the last quarter century, Phillips pointed to the stagnation or decline of real wages for most Americans—while "the share of income and wealth in the hands of the top 1 percent has risen so quickly that the United States has replaced France as the Western nation with the greatest maldistribution of wealth."

Phillips added: "The surprise really is that these trends continued under the administration of a Democrat, Bill Clinton. But in fact he, too, despite periodic Medicare and little-guy rhetoric, has played the globalization game. In this, American companies fire workers to raise their stock prices and tell employees that if wages have to keep up with inflation, they'll lose their jobs. Never mind that corporate profits are out of sight."

What is most outrageous about the Clinton administration gets bypassed in media coverage. Phillips said it well: "Almost lost in a sidebar of the ongoing Clinton-Lewinsky mess is that the first buddy, the man who ran Lewinsky's job hunt, was Washington super-fixer Vernon Jordan. Jordan and his wife Ann together hold nearly 20 corporate directorships, which may be the nationwide record. And the apparent extent to which the president and his well-wired chum share the same blue-chip economic loyalties may be the truer scandal."

February 25, 1998

When All the World's a Stage—
for Cashing In

By now, the lines between media, politics, entertainment and commercialism have just about disappeared.

This month [April 1998], Bob Dole spoke at the annual meeting of the American Association of Advertising Agencies. The former Republican presidential candidate reportedly got $40,000 for making the speech. That explains why he bothered. But why did the group invite him in the first place?

The answer is that Dole has the qualifications to address a convention of hucksters. Since leaving the Senate and the campaign trail, he has entered into a somewhat new line of work—doing commercials. His starring roles in TV spots have included pitches for such products as Dunkin' Donuts and the Visa Check Card.

Some embarrassing questions ought to arise: Are those endorsements on a par with the verities Dole spent decades proclaiming? Is he equally fervent about conservative ideology and the virtues of a glazed donut? Is he now—or has he always been—for sale?

Eager commercialism is hardly confined to the right side of the political spectrum. A couple of days before Dole's lucrative speech to assembled adsters, the famously progressive Ben and Jerry's company launched a new flavor of ice cream, "Dilbert's World."

The firm's press release was suitably euphoric. Jeanette Smith, identified as "Dilbert property manager" for United Media, set the tone: "United Media is thrilled about our partnership with Ben and Jerry's and welcome [sic] them to Dilbert's roster of more than 100 licensees."

One of those licensees is the world's largest retailer of office supplies. Animated Dilbert commercials for Office Depot are airing on network television. These days, "Shillbert" would be more like it.

Ben and Jerry's is paying a fee for the right to call its butter almond ice cream "Dilbert's World: Totally Nuts." How much? "We're not able to disclose any details of the licensing agreement," the Ben and Jerry's PR department told me.

As it happens, Dilbert creator Scott Adams is a supporter of downsizing, a position he has voiced with increasing vehemence in the past year. After an interview in November 1997, the *San Francisco Bay Guardian* reported: "The fact that corporate downsizing is good for the economy is indisputable, Adams said, adding that anybody with an IQ of more than 80 would agree."

With enough marketing momentum, it's apparently possible to work both sides of the street for a long time. So Dilbert, the icon of downtrodden office employees, is also beloved in the highest echelons of management. As *Business Week* has reported, Dilbert is a "cult hero to millions of American workers" at the same time that "CEOs hang him on the wall."

"What's next?" asks cartoonist Tom Tomorrow. "Zany Dilbert termination notices, so downsized employees can enjoy a heartfelt chuckle over the hopelessness of their plight as they're being shown the door?"

Perhaps a Ben and Jerry's flavor will be named after Ronald McDonald, with the rationale that Mr. McDonald is a symbol of the counterculture.

Irreverence that defers to big money is welcome in the mass media. For instance, Jerry Seinfeld appears in American Express commercials that he co-produces with the Ogilvy & Mather Worldwide ad agency.

Seinfeld is not reluctant. "He truly loves advertising," *Vanity Fair* magazine reports in its May [1998] issue.

"Loves" advertising?

"When any creativity becomes useful, it is sucked into the vortex of commercialism," said playwright Arthur Miller, "and when a thing becomes commercial, it becomes the enemy of man." And woman. And child.

It's not surprising that TV ads can be clever, entertaining and smoothly produced, given the huge number of dollars dumped into them. But rampant affection for this genre of media is an index of how degraded our society has become.

Underneath all the enthusiasm for the commercializing process is the notion that just about everyone and everything is for sale, or should be—that our "net worth" is what we own rather than who we are.

It's a short hop from there to nihilism. If we believe that it's appropriate to put a price tag anywhere, then we must not believe in very much of real value.

April 15, 1998

Former "Red China"
Is the Color of Money

Many of us can remember a time when "Red" seemed to be China's first name. Throughout the '50s and '60s, Red China was such a media villain that it often looked like the world's bastion of ultimate evil.

That's why, for Americans, one of the most astounding photos ever to appear on front pages was a picture of Richard Nixon and Mao shaking hands during the president's historic trip to China in February 1972.

More ice melted between the two countries after Chinese leader Deng Xiaoping gained power in the late 1970s—and promptly set a new tone with a proclamation that became an official Chinese motto. "To get rich is glorious."

For American mass media, that's an applause line.

Red China has pretty much disappeared from sight. But it's not exactly clear what is taking its place.

These days, even more than usual, the U.S. press coverage of China keeps oscillating between strong attraction and high anxiety. With its enormous population, China comes across as a beast that could be a great help or a terrible foe—a fabulous marketing opportunity or a horrendous threat.

Since America has a habit of striving to remain at the center of its own psychological universe, China routinely serves as a huge screen for American projections. "A balanced view of China as just another country—with its own pattern of development, its own problems and its own contradictions—is difficult to get from the U.S. media," Robert Weil comments.

"We're always projecting on China a role, an image," says Weil, who taught at a university in northeastern China for several months in 1993. "What I found when I went there is that, in many cases, it has very little to do with what people there are thinking or how they see the world."

Zigzagging between awed commendations and righteous condemnations of present-day China, news coverage and commentaries mirror the splits that exist in Washington. Along Pennsylvania Avenue, powerful politicians are divided on policies toward China—and U.S. media reflect those divisions.

With President Clinton visiting China [in June 1998], such ambivalence was on full display. So, while noting "the natural suspicion and swings in sentiment that always affect U.S. attitudes toward China," the June 29 issue of *Time* made sweeping statements in opposite directions.

"Chinese citizens today lead remarkably free lives, as masters of their own fates and fortunes," the magazine reported. Yet, a few sentences later, the same article declared: "Although the record is improving glacially, administration officials and human-rights observers agree it is still quite bad."

The ongoing abuse of basic human rights in China is truly horrible. Meanwhile, similar—or even more severe—repression continues in numerous U.S.-allied nations that get scant media criticism. As *Newsweek* briefly noted: "There are countries whose record on fundamental civil and religious freedom is no worse than China's; Hollywood stars have not, so far, launched a Campaign for a Free Saudi Arabia."

For the U.S. media, what's now great about China is the transformation of its economic system. A headline in *Newsweek* provided a gleeful summary: "Communism is dead. Crony capitalism lives. Today, this is a country of cell phones and pagers, McDonald's and bowling alleys." News accounts rarely mention the rampant unemployment.

Weil, who authored the recent book *Red Cat, White Cat: China and the Contradictions of "Market Socialism,"* points out that China is now undergoing "massive displacement of labor." He reels off some grim statistics.

"The official number of surplus rural laborers is an extraordinary 130 million and is rising rapidly," Weil says. "Meanwhile, in cities, there are at least 9 million unemployed and a projected 15 to 20 million more in the near future, with millions more losing wages and pensions."

Photos of Bill Clinton and Jiang Zemin shaking hands did not shock anyone. They're big men in an elite global fraternity. And you can bet that not much got lost in the translation: It's glorious to be rich.

June 24, 1998

Part VIII
Wallowing in Some Scandals, Dodging Others

"Unimpeachable Offenses"

When major news outlets and political leaders in Washington keep telling us that the same question deserves our full attention, you can bet that something is seriously amiss.

At the impeachment hearings [in December 1998], the mantra became so familiar that close observers of the performances in the Capitol theater could recite it in their sleep: Was the president guilty of an "impeachable offense"?

When a question is asked and repeated often enough, we're apt to become preoccupied with trying to answer it. And anything that sounds constitutionally profound is hard to pass up. With cable TV networks in the lead, the national media followed every twist and turn of impeachment mania.

In just about the only memorable public statement he ever made, Gerald Ford commented way back in 1970 that "an impeachable offense is whatever a majority of the House of Representatives considers it to be at a given moment in history." In other words—rhetoric aside—judgments about impeachment are ultimately subjective.

If members of Congress are able to use whatever standards they choose in evaluating presidential deeds, then you and I are entitled to the same latitude.

Although the media focus has been on "impeachable offenses," the offenses that most bother me are—evidently—unimpeachable. When journalists go on and on about putatively "impeachable offenses," the coverage distracts us from the unimpeachable ones.

As a corollary to Ford's axiom, we could say that "unimpeachable offenses" are any dastardly presidential actions that Congress refuses to view as impeachable. And when it comes to figuring out what those are, we don't have to guess.

Unlike the circumspect sages who routinely appear on such influential TV programs as the *NewsHour With Jim Lehrer*, historian Howard Zinn provides blessed relief from the fables that pass for historical perspective. His classic book *A People's*

History of the United States is a notable alternative to the texts that have long been part of schooling in America.

"I can think of at least ten reasons to impeach Clinton," says Zinn. They include the president's deceptive rationales for the attack on the religious compound in Waco, Texas, that caused eighty-one deaths; and the missile assaults on Afghanistan and Sudan [in August 1998], when the White House cited non-existent evidence that the bombed Sudanese pharmaceutical factory was producing nerve gas. [In the middle of December 1998, soon after Zinn's statement, President Clinton ordered missile bombardment of Iraq that lasted for several days.]

On the domestic front, unimpeachable offenses include the "welfare reform" that Clinton pushed into law in 1996—shoving about 1 million children below the poverty line.

No one on either side of the congressional aisle—or in the press gallery—is mentioning the "sexual McCarthyism" underway against low-income women. Gwendolyn Mink, a professor of politics at the University of California at Santa Cruz, points out that Clinton's welfare law "compels mothers to answer the government's questions about their sex lives."

This reality is news to anyone who has relied on the news media for information. "Poor unmarried mothers must tell judges or welfare officials the names of the men they have slept with if the paternity of their child has not been established," Mink explains. "In judicial proceedings, they also have had to tell how often, where and when. If they refuse, they can be denied food stamps or Medicaid or welfare. But where are the defenders of their privacy? Don't their rights count?"

The answer: Abusing thousands of poor women as a matter of policy is about as unimpeachable as any offense gets.

Of course, those sorts of concerns are absolutely not ready for impeachment prime-time. And it's a good bet that such routine moral crimes by presidents—usually committed in partnership with Congress—will remain unimpeachable.

December 9, 1998

Wading Through a Flood
of Media Clichés

Americans are up to their eyeballs in a deluge of media clichés. Ever since the Starr report became an instant classic of political pornography, news watchers have been wading through an endless flood of dubious truisms and easy platitudes.

This media tempest won't be receding any time soon, so we may as well scrutinize the popular notions that keep emerging from the spin cycle. For instance:

- "No one likes this sordid, demeaning story."

Actually, no one *admits* to liking this story. But when their ratings go through the roof, top executives at cable TV news networks are apt to be more cheerful than tearful. And quite a few print journalists have become regulars on national television, boosting their careers with prurient stories about Bill Clinton and Monica Lewinsky.

- "Newspapers did a public service by printing the full text of Kenneth Starr's report."

If so, it was a very selective public service. None of the same newspapers bothered to publish the full text of the final report by Iran-Contra independent counsel Lawrence Walsh—even though it was far more substantive.

"Ours was a constitutional question, and it dealt directly with the powers and duties of the presidency," Walsh told me in a recent interview.

Walsh's final report, released in January 1993, showed exactly how the Reagan administration had illegally sold arms to Iran—and had also broken the law by diverting funds to the Nicaraguan Contra army. The documentation was clear: In the White House and elsewhere in the executive branch, high officials conspired to violate federal statutes.

- "The American people have been shaken to learn that Clinton lied to them. He shattered the long-standing bond of trust between the public and the president."

Presidential lying is hardly new. A decade ago, President Reagan lied when he denied trading arms for hostages. As vice president and then president, George Bush lied when he kept claiming that he'd been "out of the loop" during Iran-Contra decisions.

But neither Reagan nor Bush admitted to their deceptions, which enabled U.S.-backed "freedom fighters" to function as terrorists. And no DNA tests could provide scientific proof that the blood of innocent Nicaraguan peasants was on the hands of men in the Oval Office.

- "Newt Gingrich has become a statesman, putting the good of the country above partisan concerns."

Sure. And a tiger who walks around quietly has become a vegetarian.

- "What's tragic is that Clinton could have done so much good in his second term."

Often voiced by liberals, this is an odd idea, considering the harm that Clinton did in his first term. He went all out for NAFTA and the GATT treaty that set up the World Trade Organization. He proclaimed that "the era of big government is over," undermining social programs while making the usual exception for the Pentagon. And he helped to stigmatize people on welfare as lacking "personal responsibility"—an ironic rhetorical obsession, given his own personal behavior.

- "Everybody lies about sex."

Commentators often deliver this line with some kind of smirk. But a lot of people lie about sex and a lot of people don't. Let's not further normalize deceit by claiming that "everybody" is deceitful.

- "Whether Clinton serves out his full term will depend on public opinion."

It might be more accurate to say that whether Clinton stays in office will depend on elite opinion. The public's response to the Clinton-Lewinsky scandal will probably remain mixed. If Clinton makes an early departure from the White House, it is likely to come shortly after powerful people in the realm of high finance decide that he has become too much of a problem.

- "This is the biggest presidential scandal since Watergate."

As measured by media fascination, maybe. But the statement is accurate only to the extent that the news media have done a lousy job during the last quarter of a century.

September 16, 1998

News Media Advising Clinton
on How to Spin

While preparing for his grand jury testimony, Bill Clinton got plenty of pointers—not only from lawyers and White House aides but also from the media. For weeks in mid-summer 1998, news outlets provided a crescendo of advice for the president's day of reckoning.

Some of the lead-up coverage was purposely odd, as when *Time* magazine consulted an astrologer to find out how Aug. 17 looked on Clinton's horoscope. And as a matter of routine, many journalists in Washington—no longer content to seem politically savvy—have strained to appear sexually sophisticated.

During the first half of August, a lot of reporters and pundits overtly coached Clinton on how to testify—and how to handle the media. In effect, journalists openly advised Clinton on the smoothest way to manipulate them.

This isn't exactly new. Over the past two decades, whenever the man in the Oval Office was riding high, most of the Washington press corps eagerly accommodated his deft manipulation of news media—and then cited that successful manipulation as further proof of presidential greatness. In contrast, when serious image problems arose, more and more journalists sounded like "armchair presidents."

Today, the process is more flagrant and extreme than ever. While hundreds of journalists decry Clinton's evident dishonesty as it catches up with him, a frequent media topic is the question of what he should do to extricate himself from the current crisis. Even when commentators urge him to be utterly truthful (what a concept!), the idea is usually pitched in terms of political shrewdness.

Observers have gravely counseled that some form of honesty is Clinton's best chance to finesse the mess created by his prior semi-truths and outright lies. The concerns are largely tactical. By now, the national media discourse has become so debased that honesty is just another arrow in the quiver of propaganda.

The media game of pin-the-advice-on-the-leading-donkey has become big enough for many non-journalists to play. The Aug. 17 *Newsweek* included recommendations from radio host Don Imus (Clinton is "always at his best with preacher's cadences") and a former advertising executive named Jerry Della Femina.

The magazine also supplied readers with the wisdom of erstwhile Clinton adviser Dick Morris, who wanted the president to say: "What I did was private and not political." Morris has much in common with Clinton, including boundless opportunism, notable mendacity and a historic role in creation of the 1996 welfare "reform" law that slashed federal support for America's poor children.

The *New York Times* featured an opinion piece by lawyer Nathan Lewin—who represented Edwin Meese in 1987 and 1988, during an independent-counsel probe while Meese was attorney general under President Reagan. Now, Lewin is enthusiastic about a "third option" for Clinton, beyond either "denying that he had sex with Monica Lewinsky or acknowledging that he did."

In his Aug. 12 article, Lewin considerately suggested 136 exact words for the president to use when speaking to the grand jury, beginning with: "I respectfully refuse to answer questions you are asking me, or will ask me, about my private sex life. That is none of your business, and none of any prosecutor's or investigator's business..."

As it happens, one of Clinton's top lawyers right now, Nicole Seligman, previously worked hard to defend Oliver North. According to *Newsweek*, "she's said to have the complete confidence of the First Lady." With everyone fixated on career ambitions, hired guns fit snugly into the palms of Washington's elites.

Even a broken clock is correct once in a while. And even the most powerful politician occasionally finds it convenient to tell a difficult truth.

Amid the constant media din, it takes a conscious leap to remember that the key political lies of our nation have nothing to do with sex in the White House or anywhere else.

The crucial deceptions involve the power of those with enough economic leverage to dominate Washington and severely limit democratic decision-making. Of course, we don't hear big-name journalists advising the president to speak honestly, at last, about such matters.

August 12, 1998

Sex-Scandal Coverage
Evades Clinton Contradictions

For months now, media outlets have been filled with intense debates over President Clinton's sexual conduct. But news coverage still fails to consider the Clinton scandals in the context of what he has long been preaching about welfare recipients and other low-income Americans.

So far, the mass media have shown little interest in exploring a subject that's rich with irony and potential insights—the extreme contradictions between Clinton's evident irresponsibility and his longtime insistence on tightened moral standards for the needy.

In light of his own behavior, it would be devastating for the news media to revisit the statements that Bill Clinton has made about "responsibility" ever since he began his drive for the White House at the start of this decade. Whenever Clinton trumpeted such themes, the national press corps applauded with great enthusiasm.

"Opportunity for all is not enough," Clinton declared as he fired up his presidential campaign in May 1991. "For if we give opportunity without insisting on responsibility, much of the money can be wasted and the country's strength can still be sapped. So we favor responsibility for all. That's the idea behind national service. It's the idea behind welfare reform."

The Democratic Party, Clinton proclaimed a few weeks later, "can't have people think we are captives of our own bureaucracy and that we don't recognize any responsibility on the part of the people who benefit from government programs to give something back in terms of responsible behavior."

As candidate and president, Clinton found that his repeated emphasis on requiring "responsible behavior" from welfare mothers won him accolades from a wide array of political reporters and pundits. Here, many rejoiced, was a Democrat willing to move the party away from "special interests" like poor women.

In June 1996, as President Clinton closed in on his goal of "welfare reform," he sounded a familiar theme—the ominous specter of unrestrained sexual activities. "First and foremost, community programs must stress abstinence and personal responsibility. A program cannot be successful unless it gives our children the moral leadership they need to say no to the wrong choices and yes to the right ones."

The subtexts of Clinton's rhetoric were hardly obscure. Tapping into biases among well-off whites leery of low-class sexuality, Clinton carefully aimed barbs at Americans often presumed to be dark-skinned and wanton. Implicitly, he seemed to be saying that sex was too hot for many poor people to handle. As part of the revised social contract, they would need to learn to restrain themselves.

Throughout that summer, Clinton lectured the poor. "A long time ago," he said, "I concluded that the current welfare system undermines the basic values of work, responsibility and family, trapping generation after generation in dependency and hurting the very people it was designed to help." In another speech, he proclaimed that the government should "demand responsibility from all Americans."

And when the president signed the welfare reform bill in August 1996, dumping a million children below the poverty line in the process, he was upbeat and moralistic: "Today, we are ending welfare as we know it. But I hope this day will be remembered not for what it ended, but for what it began: a new day that offers hope, honors responsibility, rewards work and changes the terms of the debate so that no one in America ever feels again the need to criticize people who are poor or on welfare."

Writing an exceptional column for *Time* magazine in late February [1998], Barbara Ehrenreich made a profound point: Clinton "signed a welfare-reform bill that, among many other regrettable things, insults the poor by providing millions for 'chastity education.' A president who snatches alms from impoverished moms while consigning their libidos to cold showers and prayer meetings, arguably deserves whatever torments await him as punishment for his own sexual derelictions."

You might think that a president whose behavior has given rise to the word "Zippergate" would provoke some media reassessment of his habitual demands that low-income Americans learn to behave responsibly. But, by and large, the news media seem to accept the idea that affluent and powerful white guys have a perfect right to tell the poor to do as they say, not as they do.

March 18, 1998

Scandal Distracts as Big Lies Persist

It has been a huge media debate—within narrow bounds.

Ever since Monica Lewinsky suddenly became a household name, the news media have been filled with fierce arguments about sex, lies and politics. Much of the coverage has focused on truth and consequences: Is President Clinton lying about his relationship with the former White House intern? Should it matter?

These are the kinds of questions that the media establishment loves. They can be debated endlessly, with appreciable entertainment value. And—since any individual politician is expendable—no really powerful interests are going to mind very much.

There's plenty of emphasis on revealing whether or not particular men and women in Washington are telling the truth about their behavior. But only some truth seems to be important. When it comes to policies that have been matters of life and death, the standard media deceptions continue—raising few eyebrows along the way.

A week after it beat the competition by splashing the Lewinsky story on its front page, the *Washington Post* published an editorial urging the U.S. government to release information about dealings with a murderous death squad in Honduras during the 1980s: "The emerging outlines of this affair indicate that the United States, in working with the Honduran military to support anti-Communist forces in El Salvador and Nicaragua, set up a special 'Battalion 3-16' to 'monitor and destroy…subversives' in Honduras."

That was straightforward enough. But the *Post* went on to place its concerns in a remarkable context. "The United States went to the Central American wars to protect and build local democracies," the newspaper declared. "That project did not stop when the wars were over."

The statement is a lie. In the 1980s, the United States went to the Central American wars to protect enemies of democracy who were aligned with landed aristocracies and other economic elites. *That* project did not stop when the wars were over.

If journalism is the first draft of history, we might expect later drafts to improve. Not so. The revisions do little to enhance accuracy. In fact, the adherence to official lies may become more fixed over time.

The assumption in mainstream American media is that Washington's foreign policies are benign in intent, if not always in effect. Somehow, whatever the criticisms, U.S. government policy-makers are routinely depicted as well-meaning.

Often, the lies our media tell us are smooth as silence, with key facts downplayed or omitted entirely. No one need be the wiser.

So it was in a recent *New York Times* editorial essay. "A quarter-century after the coup that overthrew Salvador Allende," the Jan. 20 [1998] article noted, "General Augusto Pinochet is still poisoning Chile's public life." The piece went on to recount that Pinochet's regime "killed or tortured thousands of people" after he and other military officers toppled the democratically elected Chilean government.

But the essay, by *Times* writer Tina Rosenberg, was a story with much of the actual plot missing. In the real world, the U.S. government played a pivotal role—actively backing the 1973 coup that brought Pinochet and his bloody henchmen to power.

In the world according to the *New York Times*, however, the U.S. government was a bit player, scarcely worth mentioning. The essay's only reference to the United States was fleeting and oblique: "Under Mr. Allende, Chileans never knew if school was open or if they could buy bread. The chaos, intensified by the Nixon administration's efforts to undermine Mr. Allende, was profoundly disturbing to most of Chile."

Does it matter how the past is portrayed by news outlets? Yes. The illusions that surround us are like thick fog: blurring what has already occurred, what is happening now and what is on the horizon.

George Orwell's timeworn adage from his novel *1984* bears repeating: "Who controls the past controls the future; who controls the present controls the past."

Transfixing the nation with the Lewinsky saga, the news media have not in the least threatened the big-money corporate interests that dominate Washington—and will continue to do so, whatever the fate of the Clinton presidency.

February 4, 1998

How Bush Got a
Golden Parachute From Moon

When George Bush jumped out of an airplane one day in the spring of 1997, his sky-diving feat was big news. But this country's media outlets have failed to inform the public about far more important activities by the former president.

Four months before his leap with a parachute, Bush traveled to South America—where he provided a major boost for the launch of a newspaper that belongs to the Rev. Sun Myung Moon.

Since leaving the White House, Bush has been quite helpful to Moon. However, the news media have lacked curiosity about Bush's ties to the shadowy power broker who heads the Unification Church. Moon's global empire combines cult-like authority over "Moonies" with extensive media holdings.

"President Bush has no relationship with Rev. Moon or the Unification Church," Bush spokesman Jim McGrath assured me in a recent interview. But the facts tell a very different story.

On Nov. 23, 1996, Bush walked to the podium at the Sheraton Hotel in Buenos Aires and delivered a speech to 900 guests invited by Moon to celebrate the opening of his regional daily paper, *Tiempos del Mundo*. As Moon beamed a few feet away, Bush lauded his host.

"I want to salute Rev. Moon, who is the founder of the *Washington Times* and also of *Tiempos del Mundo*," Bush said. He praised the Washington newspaper for fostering "sanity"—and added that Moon's new paper in Argentina "is going to do the same thing."

The fifteen-year-old *Washington Times* doesn't rank among the top 100 U.S. dailies in terms of circulation. Yet, financed by the Unification Church's deep pockets, it wields enormous influence in the nation's capital. Elevating innuendo into "news," the paper excels at smearing liberals and centrists.

During the last couple of years, Bush has spoken at high-profile Moon events on three continents. He went to Asia in September 1995, giving several speeches for a group led by Moon's wife, Hak Ja Han Moon. In Tokyo, Bush addressed a gathering of 50,000 Moon followers. Ten months later, in Washington, Bush spoke at a Moon-sponsored conference.

Instead of growing, press attention to the Bush-Moon links has gone from scant to almost non-existent. Bush's role in Buenos Aires barely got reported in the United States.

But in August [1997], former *Newsweek* correspondent Robert Parry shines some light with an extensive report, "The Dark Side of Rev. Moon." It's appearing in *I.F. Magazine*, a new periodical named in memory of the late journalists I.F. Stone and George Seldes (the editor of the muckraking newsletter *In fact*).

A few samples of Parry's findings:

- Prior to the première of *Tiempos del Mundo*, much of the Latin American press was hostile to the newspaper project. But Bush's ringing endorsement allayed some concerns about Moon's ownership. In the words of a Unification Church bulletin, "Mr. Bush's presence as keynote speaker gave the event invaluable prestige."

- Although Bush won't disclose how much money he has received from Moon-affiliated organizations, Parry reports that "estimates of Bush's fee for the Buenos Aires appearances alone ran between $100,000 and $500,000. Sources close to the Unification Church have put the total Bush-Moon package in the millions." According to one source, Bush's net could be as high as $10 million.

- Bush's lucrative courtship of Moon may help the ex-president to lay groundwork for his son George W. Bush, the current governor of Texas, who is expected to run for the next Republican presidential nomination.

- "A silent testimony to Moon's clout," Parry writes, "is the fact that his vast spending of billions of dollars in secretive Asian money to influence U.S. politics—spanning nearly a quarter-century—has gone virtually unmentioned amid the current controversy over Asian donations to U.S. politicians."

(If you'd like to read Robert Parry's fine reporting in *I.F. Magazine,* call 1-800-738-1812 or visit the website at www.consortiumnews.com.)

What Moon seeks to accomplish with his riches is chilling to consider. As Frederick Clarkson's book *Eternal Hostility* explains, Unification Church operatives "have been close to neo-fascist movements all over the world."

Here in the United States, it remains to be seen whether the national media will finally focus on the Rev. Sun Myung Moon and his tacit alliance with George Bush.

An important question about American journalism hovers in the air: Who's afraid of the Rev. Moon?

July 30, 1997

Part IX
Selective Spinning for Politicians

This Is Your Media Life, Bill Clinton!

Ten years ago, few Americans knew your name. Today, many wish they could forget it. This is your media life, Bill Clinton!

When you jumped onto the national stage with peppy rhetoric about moving beyond the ideologies of left and right, you impressed mainstream news outlets. A lot of journalists wanted a "New Democrat," and you did the trick.

While making some mild populist noises, you curried favor with big-business leaders who fretted about anti-corporate rumblings among Democrats. Months before you won the presidency, numerous reporters and pundits were hailing you as JFK: The Next Generation.

After you moved into the White House, of course, scandals became abundant—but you proved to be a great counterpuncher inside the media ring. More importantly, with a wide range of policies, you pleased many economic heavyweights.

Meanwhile, you showed enthusiasm for betraying longtime Democratic constituencies. And in 1996, you succeeded where the GOP had failed for several decades, taking a major step toward dismantling the New Deal with a welfare "reform" law that undermined federal commitments to America's poor children.

In January 1998, when Monica Lewinsky suddenly became famous, you went into damage-control overdrive. You benefited from the fact that many liberal commentators—repulsed by the sleazy tactics of Kenneth Starr and the far right—went easy on you.

By early August, pathetic excuses were so routine that few eyebrows seemed to go up when Arthur Schlesinger Jr. declared in a *New York Times* essay: "Gentlemen always lie about their sex lives. Only a cad will tell the truth about his sexual affairs."

Overall, you and your avid defenders have done the virtually impossible—making some top Republicans in Congress look like seekers of truth. It's an optical illusion. But you became the perfect foil for every right-wing moralizer from San Diego to Bangor.

When you were forced to admit that you'd lied about "that woman," your brief speech was so cravenly evasive that you became, more than ever, a poster boy for duplicity. You functioned as an ultimate media creature—smarmy and indignant, pious and pugilistic—once again a fountain of weasel-worded clichés and a champion of not one firm principle.

In the process, you've helped the news media to accelerate in the same direction they were headed anyway—fixating the nation on a convoluted soap opera plot instead of genuine political discourse. The spectacle is unfolding as some kind of mass hypnosis.

Since your mini-speech on Aug. 17 [1998], media brickbats have been flying thick and fast. Let that be a lesson to you: These days, if presidential lies extend to sexual activities inside the White House, you're liable to get heavy media censure.

In contrast, if you stick to the usual deceptions—such as advancing the interests of the wealthy at the expense of poor and middle-class Americans—you can relax, confident that media criticisms will be muted and scattered.

Of course, media self-examination has been on display. Fortunately for the big-money interests that have been pleased with your economic priorities, such introspection doesn't go very deep.

Two nights after your semi-apologetic little speech, the *NewsHour With Jim Lehrer* aired a segment about media coverage of the current scandal. It was a product of the PBS program's special new unit for examining media behavior—made possible by a $3 million grant from the Pew Charitable Trusts and headed by former CBS News correspondent Terence Smith.

The *NewsHour* presented a lengthy discussion between Smith and three other media insiders: the Washington bureau chiefs of the *Los Angeles Times* and CNN, plus former *LA Times* reporter Tom Rosenstiel, who's now director of the Project for Excellence in Journalism. Viewers weren't told that Rosenstiel's project is financed by Pew, the same multibillion-dollar outfit generously funding Smith and the *NewsHour*. It was all very cozy—and typical.

So, Bill Clinton, beyond tragedy and farce, you remain a figment of our national non-imagination. Despite all the uproar, your longtime corporate backers are not worried about the news media getting out of hand. You may sink beneath the political waves, but the Fortune 500 will stay high and dry.

August 19, 1998

Bumpy Media Road
for a Presidential Drive

During the last quarter-century, many journalists have portrayed the Democratic Party as an uneasy mix of pragmatic moderates, unrealistic liberals and stubborn leftists. With attention now turning to the party's next presidential nomination, such media themes will soon be surging again.

Al Gore is the party's heir apparent. Most of the Washington press corps seem to like the vice president, who blends mild social liberalism with fierce loyalty to corporate power. Generally speaking, he's their kind of guy.

Sen. Paul Wellstone is not their kind of guy. While running for a second term in 1996, he voted against the cruel welfare "reform" bill that President Clinton pushed into law. Commentators quickly wrote Wellstone's political obituary. Back home in Minnesota, his Republican foe denounced "Senator Welfare." But Wellstone—with extensive grassroots support—defied the gods of mass media and won re-election to the Senate.

Today, Paul Wellstone is saying that he wants to run for president in 2000. And you can almost hear the mainstream pundits sharpening their knives.

A classic sequence of media spin is probable if Wellstone goes ahead with a presidential campaign: First, he can't win. Then, if he makes headway in early primaries and caucuses, he shouldn't win. And if a lot of voters keep rejecting that assessment, then the hue and cry will be that his nomination would wreck the Democratic Party.

Writing about a possible Wellstone race, syndicated columnists Ben and Daniel Wattenberg scoffed that the senator's distinguishing political characteristics include the fact that he is "antiquely" in favor of federal jobs programs.

But thoroughly modern pundits may not denigrate the value of "message candidates"—at least during the he-can't-win phase. "Their circuit rides bring fresh ideas, new voters and new activists into the system," the neo-conservative Wattenbergs exulted. "In fact, such candidacies may have replaced third parties as the safety valve of American politics. More voters feel represented, fewer feel alienated."

That sort of backhanded praise for a long-shot presidential campaign is meant as a fleeting pat on the head. But it may actually point to a drawback of progressive efforts to win the Democratic presidential nomination.

The purpose of fighting for genuine political change and an end to corporate dominance, after all, is not to make more voters "feel" represented. In the high places where key decisions are made, with so many profound consequences, we should *be* represented.

In the continued absence of real representation, it might not be an improvement if "fewer feel alienated." In a country where huge gaps are widening between the rich and the rest of us—in terms of money and power—we need major transformations of economic structures, not safety valves.

But when presidential campaigns heat up, we hear plenty of specious media talk about "special interests."

In mediaspeak, the special interests usually include unionized workers, African Americans, low-income people and seniors. Yet Wall Street and large corporations are presumed to represent the national interest.

In this media context, any politician who fights the power of the party system can expect to be depicted as an interloper.

Ten years ago, in the sweltering summer heat of Atlanta, I spoke with people who had come to the Democratic National Convention from all over the country as delegates for Jesse Jackson. Earlier in 1988, during the primaries, Jackson had won 7.5 million Democratic votes, about 30 percent of all ballots cast. But media coverage often went to great lengths to portray Jackson as a party crasher, intruding where he didn't belong.

At the '88 convention, where Michael Dukakis prevailed, Jackson urged that the platform call for freezing taxes on the middle class and poor while only hiking taxes on wealthy individuals and corporations. Journalists routinely described it simply as a plan for higher taxes. When the Jackson plank went down to defeat, many pundits hailed a victory over "special interests."

Now, as Paul Wellstone hits the national campaign trail— speaking about the imperative need to provide all Americans with "a good education, good health care and a good job"— he may not appeal to elites. But a lot of other people will be listening.

[In January 1999, Paul Wellstone announced that he would not run for president in 2000.]

July 15, 1998

Five Years Into the Clinton Presidency

Later this month, as Bill Clinton completes his fifth year in the White House, the press is likely to tell us—at great length—what his presidency has meant so far. But don't expect much scrutiny of the news media's role in the Clinton era.

When the incoming president took the oath of office on Jan. 20, 1993, it was a dream come true for many journalists. They had long bemoaned the failure of the Democratic Party to restrain so-called "special interests." At last, the New Democrats triumphed—pushing low-income people and other vulnerable Americans to the back of the political bus. Most of the punditocracy beamed.

Since then, Clinton's willingness to shaft faithful constituencies of the party has won him more friends in high places. To the applause of numerous commentators, he went to the mat repeatedly on behalf of economic elites—eager for such measures as pro-business trade pacts, bailouts overseas and harsh "welfare reform" at home.

As 1998 gets underway, some revised media clichés are ready for the next phase of the Clinton presidency: Despite all the scandals, he remains popular. Buoyed by popularity, he lacks purpose.

President Clinton "has given Americans no vision of where the country ought to be going," *New York Times* columnist Anthony Lewis lamented in his last commentary of 1997. Such hand-wringing is common—particularly among liberal pundits.

If this president were a Republican, they'd be a bit more inclined to denounce his policies and decry his well-honed talent for dissembling. But he's a Democrat—and has withstood years of vicious attacks from right-wing Republicans who, in many cases, have engaged in distortions for their own purposes. Clinton's enemies "are so hateful that they have created a certain public sympathy for him," Lewis noted.

Yes, Jerry Falwell and some others on the far right have put out a barrage of lies about Clinton. But that doesn't make Clinton a virtuous president. While clear-eyed assessments of the Clinton administration are in short supply, the news media provide us with a lot of evasive pieties.

In his widely syndicated column, Lewis ended 1997 with these words: "The poison directed at President Clinton goes along with the attacks on all of government as evil. The coin of our politics is being corrupted, and it is hard to see what will restore civic discourse and enable us to deal with the country's real problems."

Meanwhile, there's substantial evidence that Bill Clinton *does* have a vision for the country. It is similar to the vision he has pursued for himself: Opportunism. Duplicity. Ultra-pragmatism.

These inclinations are apt to be familiar to the many reporters, editors and pundits who feel that career advancement is extremely important. Idealism might sound good, but expediency is shrewd.

What mainstream journalists have rarely pointed out—perhaps because so many of them are part of the process—is that President Clinton has helped to normalize deceit and narcissism during the 1990s. This tells us something about the Clinton presidency. But it tells us more about the national press corps.

There are, of course, journalists who march to the beats of different drummers. Some are independent thinkers willing to go against the dominant grain. Some try their best to serve humanistic values in the workplace. But the obstacles and constraints are enormous. And the exceptional feats are dwarfed by the spinning machinery of the mass media.

One of the great flaws of American media coverage has been its emphasis on the personal psychodramas of the man in the Oval Office. With inordinate amounts of attention devoted to personalizing each presidency, the political horizons of the country seem to be overshadowed by a never-ending procession of historic individuals.

Yet, as media critic Mark Crispin Miller has observed, "this image of the mighty individual is a corporate fiction, the careful work of committees and think tanks, repeatedly reprocessed by the television industry for daily distribution to a mass audience."

What's profound about any presidential quest is how it affects the people of this country and the entire world. That's easy for journalists—and the rest of us—to forget.

[This column appeared three weeks before the Monica Lewinsky scandal broke.]

December 31, 1997

Part X
Confining by Race

Diagnosis for News Media: "Diversity Fatigue"

A new term for an old problem has just emerged in the national press. We're now told that much of the media industry has come down with "diversity fatigue."

Before this malady, the story goes, the American Society of Newspaper Editors was committed to racial diversity. Back in 1978, the group set a goal of "achieving minority employment at daily newspapers that matches minority representation in the general U.S. population by the year 2000, or sooner."

Twenty years ago, when the editors did a nationwide survey, they found that only 4 percent of staffers were black, Latino, Asian or Native American. Today, the numbers look better—11.4 percent—but hardly impressive. After all, fully one-quarter of the American public is composed of racial minorities.

Never swift, the progress stalled during the 1990s. At this rate, the editors' group will miss its announced deadline by about a century.

Of course, the American Society of Newspaper Editors could choose to redouble its efforts. Instead, ASNE has proposed dumping the goal in favor of less ambitious targets. Daunted by its own inertia, the newspaper industry is pleading exhaustion.

Media outlets, whether daily papers or broadcast networks, face many challenges. When it comes to battling for market share, there's no sign of fatigue. When it's a matter of struggling for a big profit margin, their eyes are always on the prize. But somehow, when racial equity is at stake, weariness is too overwhelming.

The media establishment continues to summon a great deal of energy for boosting the bottom line. But the top honchos are oh so tired of the quest for racial equality.

Let's give credit where due: A lot of media managers can be innovative and tenacious. The colorful arrival of *USA Today* in the 1980s, for instance, spurred hundreds of daily papers to bring color to their newsprint with eye-pleasing design makeovers. Frequently, presses were junked or modernized at a cost of many millions of dollars.

But diversifying the color of people in the newsrooms rarely got that kind of priority. Some sincere editors and managers, as well as reporters, pushed to bolster minority hiring. Yet perhaps the burden has worn out its welcome.

If the nation's top editors were as committed to profitability as they've been to racial balance, most media companies would have gone bankrupt a long time ago.

Ironically, the retreating sounds from the American Society of Newspaper Editors came just after the thirtieth anniversary of the Kerner Commission Report on the causes of urban riots.

The 1968 commission didn't simply call for integrating the ranks of newspaper reporters, who were almost all white at the time. The panel stressed the need for minorities in decision-making positions: "Newspaper and television policies are, generally speaking, not set by reporters. Editorial decisions about which stories to cover and which to use are made by editors."

These days, so-called diversity fatigue seems to be widespread. After many years of bashing from pundits and politicians, affirmative action is on the ropes. One result: University of California campuses are now seeing a sharp drop in applications and admissions of black and Latino students.

Whether in the media business, colleges or other institutions, whites often embrace the illusion that people can transcend racism by ignoring it. But this "colorblind" approach has a way of being blind to the power of racism in the present day.

Many editors seem notably patient about racism, while patience with measures like affirmative action has declined or disappeared.

"Diversity fatigue" is a rather euphemistic way to describe the process. If you peer through the foggy evasions, you might catch a glimpse of white supremacy: more subtle than decades ago but still very powerful. No wonder so many Americans, in their hearts, are suffering from racism fatigue.

April 8, 1998

Honoring King While Clouding His Legacy

Whether by design or a random twist of fate, President Clinton's return to Washington from his historic Africa trip came just before the 30th anniversary of the death of Martin Luther King Jr.

Another laudatory statement from the White House was predictable. Like countless other politicians, Clinton often pays tribute to King—while selectively praising his legacy.

But imagine the media uproar if Clinton had stepped off Air Force One and proceeded to quote some of King's less palatable assertions.

For instance, in a speech exactly one year before he was assassinated on April 4, 1968, King declared: "A true revolution of values will soon look uneasily on the glaring contrast of poverty and wealth." And he denounced "capitalists of the West investing huge sums of money in Asia, Africa and South America, only to take the profits out with no concern for the social betterment of the countries."

The mass media and both major parties have no use for this sort of talk. They like the safe images of King as a great orator, a brave civil-rights leader, a martyr on a postage stamp.

King's denunciations of predatory investments in the Third World may seem outdated or exaggerated. After all, journalists and pundits frequently tell us, investments from abroad are key to the uplift of poor nations, especially in this era of economic globalization.

But the truth is more complex—and the continent that President Clinton just visited is a prime example. You wouldn't know it from the usual media coverage, but foreign investors have brought widespread calamities to Africa.

The popular myth is that the West has poured humanitarian aid into Africa. But actually, more money is flowing *out* of Africa than into it. The reason? "Debt service"—the loan repayments, including interest and portions of the principal, required by banks and other lenders.

"Africa actually pays out more than four times as much on debt servicing…than it spends on education and health services," scholar Deborah L. Toler reports in the April [1998] issue of *Essence* magazine.

"Western economic exploitation continues through unfair trade practices and enforcement of crushing debt burdens," Toler writes. That's an update on the kind of analysis that Martin Luther King offered during his final years. It wasn't welcomed by U.S. news media then, and it doesn't seem to be any more appreciated now.

Like many other researchers and activists, Toler is highly critical of the World Bank and the International Monetary Fund—which, she contends, "are responsible for the economic hardships behind many conflicts in Africa today. To repay these two international lenders of last resort for loans taken out in the '70s and '80s, many countries have cut expenses on social services like schools and health clinics, and they've downsized by eliminating civil-service jobs."

What's more, Toler says, the lenders have undermined local agriculture: "Loan-repayment programs also force African governments to emphasize exporting to earn the foreign exchange to repay their loans. Trouble is, the emphasis on exports means less focus on growing food for local consumption, and small farmers are being pushed onto fragile lands where crop yields suffer."

The news media have carried many tributes to Dr. King. Mostly, they stress his quest for racial equality—but shed little light on the challenge to economic injustice that increasingly preoccupied him.

Decrying enormous income gaps, King called for "radical changes in the structure of our society" to redistribute wealth and power. During his last months, he was organizing the Poor People's Campaign, "a multiracial army of the poor" that would converge on Washington. He accused Congress of "hostility to the poor"—appropriating "military funds with alacrity and generosity" but providing "poverty funds with miserliness."

"The time has come for us to civilize ourselves by the total, direct and immediate abolition of poverty," King said in early 1968. But in 1998, the big media outlets that trumpet his "dream" aren't repeating such words. Whether in Africa or America, the powerful have a very different agenda.

April 1, 1998

M. WUERKER

A Big Story Goes Unreported: White Delusion

Despite all the news coverage of race in this country, there's very little media attention to a serious hazard that white people face. In a word: delusion.

Today, three out of four Americans remain at risk—susceptible to frequent intimations that they're superior because they're white. Sunscreen is a big seller, but there isn't a product available to protect against the implicit touting of whiteness as a virtue.

Whites receive plenty of reinforcement for the conceit that the color of their skin somehow makes them smarter and better. Although messages of that sort have become more subtle in recent decades, a lot of media images and political rhetoric still encourage belief in such fantasies.

If newsrooms and media suites weren't so overwhelmingly white, this situation might be more widely—and forthrightly—discussed in print and on the airwaves. Perhaps some pundits would voice concern about "white pathology" and wonder aloud at the extent of moral failures by Caucasians who live in the outer city.

But as things stand, we don't hear much about the social sickness involved in the propensity of white commentators to confuse their monologues with real dialogue on the subject of race.

Affirmative action is a flash point for the unspoken—and often unconscious—white delusion of superiority. We're commonly told that affirmative action is now unnecessary because a level playing field exists.

Out of touch with reality, these claims ignore the fact that racial prejudice and institutional bias continue to pervade American society—and that few blacks or Latinos can be found in the more lucrative and powerful professions. Given the lopsided statistics, the level-playing-field argument doesn't hold—unless, of course, one actually believes that racial minorities are inherently inferior.

A new twist in the debate contends that affirmative action isn't worth fighting for. Early this fall [1997], in the liberal *Mother Jones* magazine, Editor in Chief Jeffrey Klein declared that "we need to admit that affirmative action has failed as a long-term political strategy" and "has eroded liberals' moral credibility as reformers."

Writing an introductory essay for a collection of articles on "America's Changing Colors," Klein explained that the topic's importance caused the magazine to devote "so much of this issue to rethinking race." But the rethinking was rather limited, as were the experiences and outlooks of the rethinkers.

While they appeared under the heading of "America's Changing Colors," all five of the articles were written by whites. That helps explain why, on one page after another, blacks and Latinos and Asian Americans come across as little more than political chips to be moved by white hands.

In the process of urging progressive people to discard affirmative action as a loser, *Mother Jones* itself displayed the causes and consequences of such a mentality: An all-white editorial hierarchy decided to publish a cluster of articles exploring race in America, written only by white people.

But apparently, Klein is untroubled by the magazine's position. He told me that although "as a transitional program it did a lot of good," now affirmative action "is a bad course to be going down."

Klein sounded satisfied with the special issue on race. "We've gotten a mixed positive response," he said. And he added: "The issue seems to be selling extremely well."

In media outlets, the results are grim when white people are presented as the arbiters of public discourse on race. Those who aren't white tend to fade into abstraction as "the other"—talked about extensively and heard from occasionally.

And so continues the dominant and ponderous white monologue on America's racial conflicts.

THE HABITS OF HIGHLY DECEPTIVE MEDIA

Two years ago, *Village Voice* media critic James Ledbetter wrote a series called "The Unbearable Whiteness of Publishing." Its conclusions are even more relevant now: "Under the best of circumstances, the print media's domination by whites would be a stain of dishonor. In today's political climate, the persistence of whiteness leaves the press ill-equipped to raise persuasive challenges to the accelerating attack on civil rights."

[In late summer 1998, under pressure, Jeffrey Klein resigned as editor in chief of *Mother Jones*.]

October 8, 1997

Black Women Confined in Media Cage

In medialand, some people have every right to be angry. So we see affluent white guys on television all the time, expounding views forcefully, letting us all know what they like—and what makes them mad.

Black women are another matter entirely. Sure, they're visible on quite a few commercials. And MTV's music videos don't lack for stereotyped black babes dancing to hot tunes. But African-American females have little chance to speak out about their daily lives and deepest concerns.

It's still conspicuous when a black woman gets the microphone to talk about what matters to her. And it's rarer still for major media to provide a substantial amount of time and space for black women to talk about the combination of racism, sexism and economic disadvantage that they face in this society.

In sharp contrast, vehemence from white men isn't just acceptable—it's valued if it lets us in on authoritative outlooks. Strong statements of opinion, uttered with commanding presence in mainstream media outlets, are routine for the punditocracy. Bombastic TV programs like *The Capital Gang* and *The McLaughlin Group* showcase men who vent their biases.

While the rage of white males is part of the media landscape, the rage of black women—who have plenty to be angry about—gets cut off at the media pass. That's why it's especially meaningful that journalist Jill Nelson is now doing an end run around the usual blockade.

When I interviewed Nelson halfway through a month-long national tour for her new book *Straight, No Chaser*, she was in the midst of burning up the radio waves across the country—helping to force key issues into the open.

Subtitled *How I Became a Grown-up Black Woman*, the book insists that silence—far from being golden—is corrosive. Urging that the unhealthy quiet be shattered, Nelson follows her own advice by mincing no words:

- "The culture that we consume through television, magazines, and advertisements confirms our lack of importance." Black women "are totally absent from all serious political discussion. Even during February, Black History Month, black men are the preferred race representatives. March, Women's History Month, is for white women only."

- "Entertainment? Forget it. Even though black Americans watch more free network television than anyone else, there is not a single dramatic show on television about black women, much less a black woman producing one."

- "When it comes to beauty, the preoccupation of women's magazines and women's programming, we are definitely not up to snuff. We're too dark, big-boned, our features too Negroid, too ethnic-looking, in short, too much black women, to even qualify to enter America's beauty sweepstakes."

- "The result of black women's silence in the face of the verbiage of others is we find ourselves further misrepresented, erased, excluded. Those who demonize us and call for [social-program] cuts are usually white men who do not know a single black woman. If they do, she's probably a domestic employee."

- "It's hard to hold on to your humanity, your ability to love, when the national psyche is so profoundly invested in defining black people as always part of the problem, rarely part of the solution."

- "The affirmation, strength, and voice that black women desperately need must initially come from ourselves and other black women, those who share our experiences... Those who don't define themselves are doomed to be defined by others, erased, or, as is the case with black women, both."

Don't look for Jill Nelson on the national TV programs where irate white guys keep pounding away at favorite themes like "welfare dependency" among low-income single mothers. Those blowhards don't have to contend with articulate black women who could shine a fierce light on their assorted bigotries. The dominant media pundits want to go up against "opposition" that's meek and mild—and, as usual in medialand, they get their way.

September 24, 1997

A Media Malady:
Image Distortion Disorder

Are we suffering from Image Distortion Disorder?

It's not listed in medical dictionaries. But physician Michael LeNoir is urging our society to treat Image Distortion Disorder as a very real—and very unhealthy—condition.

Possible remedies aren't discussed on television. Instead of helping to alleviate Image Distortion Disorder, prime time is ablaze with programming that inflames it.

This is a pervasive ailment that has no obvious physical symptoms. It stokes fears and antagonisms so familiar that they're apt to seem natural.

"Most of the images that one ethnic group has of another are developed by the media," Dr. LeNoir has observed. And media images have a way of feeding on themselves. "The incessant portrayal of African Americans as criminals and buffoons has been responsible for the success of many police programs and sitcoms."

The white majority remains ill-informed. "Most people in America get their information about people of color from radio, movies, print and especially television," LeNoir notes. "In most instances, people of color are depicted as drug-addicted, homeless, child-abusing, welfare criminals."

LeNoir, an African American who practices medicine in Oakland, California, is calling for "more realistic images of our young people." He adds: "Most of them graduate from high school, do not go to prison and enter the work force in significant numbers."

A new study confirms that media outlets keep applying blackface to this nation's afflictions. Only 29 percent of poor Americans are black—but when Yale University scholar Martin Gilens examined coverage of poverty in national news magazines like *Time* and *Newsweek*, he found that 62 percent of the pictures were of blacks. On network TV evening newscasts, the figure was 65 percent.

"Part of the problem is news professionals to some degree share the same misperceptions that the public does," Gilens commented. "The people who are choosing the photographs sort of misunderstand the social realities."

Whether the issue is poverty, crime or drugs, the tilt of the media mirror often makes racial minorities look bad. In Dr. LeNoir's words, "the perception painted by television of people of color becomes the reality, and it creates a background of anxiety and fear in America that is dangerous."

Writing in a fine new anthology titled *Multi-America*, LeNoir asserts that media distortions of African Americans, Latinos and Asians "have a devastating effect on every person in this country and undermine any attempt to bring us together as a people."

He emphasizes the importance of speaking up: "Those of us in America who are concerned about race relations must react to obvious distortions in the media by raising our voices in protest over the never-ending attempt to portray people of color in these caricatured, fragmented and distorted images."

It's symbolic that the book containing LeNoir's essay on Image Distortion Disorder has gotten the cold shoulder from mass media—despite the fact that it is a landmark volume put out by a major publisher (Viking) and edited by a prominent author (Ishmael Reed).

Multi-America is a collection of pieces by Americans whose ancestors came from Asia, Africa and Latin America in addition to European countries such as Italy and Ireland. The book demolishes stereotypes while challenging the traditional, monocultural view of what it means to be "an American."

Key media outlets, ranging from *Publishers Weekly* to the *New York Times*, have refused to review *Multi-America*. Perhaps the 465-page hardcover book—featuring eloquent essays by more than 50 American writers from a wide array of ethnic and racial backgrounds—would have seemed more valuable if those writers had been at each other's throats.

Meanwhile, the Little, Brown publishing house, owned by Time Warner, has shelled out a $3 million advance for yet another book about O.J. Simpson, this one by former girlfriend Paula Barbieri. Her book, of course, will get massive media attention. Sounds like another victory for Image Distortion Disorder.

August 20, 1997

Part XI
Fixating on Fame

Teen People
and the Souls of Young Folks

People magazine now has a clone. The first issue of *Teen People*—a slick monthly "from the editors of *People*"—just hit newsstands across the country.

It's colorful. Stylish. And disturbing.

Much of the new magazine is focused on female images. Profuse advertising begins on the inside front cover, with fold-out pages of girls in tight Gap jeans. Dozens of big ads follow, offering brand-name clothes, cosmetics, fragrances and skin creams.

"L'Oreal," says the headline under a woman's face at the start of a multi-page spread. "Because I'm worth it." Such pitches may sound affirming. Yet they're insidious—linking a person's worth to what she buys and how she looks.

That's good for marketers. But what about adolescents?

American girls routinely experience a sharp drop in self-esteem as they become teenagers. Appearance and social approval are apt to loom large. Fitting in—with a fashionable wardrobe and slim waist—can seem to be imperative.

Sadly, the emergence of this new magazine is liable to make things worse. Instead of opening the world for adolescent readers, *Teen People* narrows it. Glossy pages equate excitement with glamorous stars of the entertainment industry. Joys are vicarious. The top story on *Teen People*'s first cover sums it up: "Celeb Couples Share Their Love Secrets."

The premier issue of *Teen People* does include a few substantive articles. But whatever value they might have is undermined by the rest of the magazine.

A story about the brutal rituals of a college fraternity, "Dying to Belong," warns of binge drinking and "rampant hard-core hazing" on campuses. It's a well-done article that depicts an extreme form of peer pressure. But it appears in a magazine that relies on peer pressure to sell its wares.

Another feature praises virginity among teenagers. "Waiting can be a cool choice," the magazine advises. Yet many of the ads and photos in *Teen People* are highly sexualized. All the better to hook readers and hawk products.

The debut issue of *Teen People* also devotes four pages to a major problem—the alarming rates of eating disorders among American females. The article warns against obsession with weight. "The whole dieting mentality is exactly what leads to severe cases of anorexia and bulimia," says one expert.

Teen People sounds a cautionary note: "It can be all too easy for some girls to get sucked into the warped social scene of competitive dieting or the greater extreme of group bingeing and purging." But the article is totally silent about the fact that much of our society's dangerous emphasis on thinness comes from media outlets.

Unfortunately, media images that glorify thin as beautiful—sometimes to the point of emaciation—are well represented in the pages of *Teen People*. Quite a few of the magazine's ads display skinny young women gazing into the camera.

Readers of *Teen People* will learn what they need—or, more precisely, what merchandisers want them to feel they need. The magazine is just the latest addition to the portfolio of Time Warner, the world's largest media corporation. The firm expects *Teen People*'s formula to boost revenues from advertisers.

In a book titled *Ways of Seeing*, published a quarter of a century ago, John Berger denounced the shallow mania for publicity that limits so many dreams: "It recognizes nothing except the power to acquire. All other human faculties or needs are made subsidiary to this power. All hopes are gathered together, made homogeneous, simplified, so that they become the intense yet vague, magical yet repeatable promise offered in every purchase."

Publicity, wrote Berger, "turns consumption into a substitute for democracy. The choice of what one eats (or wears or drives) takes the place of significant political choice. Publicity helps to mask and compensate for all that is undemocratic within society."

Berger made that complaint in 1972. *People* magazine was founded two years later. Since then, the glamorizing of individual fame has continued to escalate. Today, with 38 million readers every week, *People* calls itself "the most successful magazine in the world."

Teen People is now being touted as "the first general interest publication for teens that celebrates their diverse lifestyles and wide array of interests." Sounds like progress. But it isn't.

January 7, 1998

Good Grief: When It Reigns, It Pours

During the weeks since the death of Princess Diana, a variety of news outlets have commented on the startling importance of emotions. Jolted by intense public mourning, many reporters now proclaim that human feelings matter—a lot.

"As a journalist, I've long avoided feelings," news analyst Daniel Schorr confessed to National Public Radio listeners. "I used to consider thoughts important and feelings irrelevant. No longer. Gradually, it's been brought home to me that feelings may have more validity than opinions."

Kept under wraps or unleashed, feelings have always made a big difference. The problem is that emotional reactions—whether masked by cerebral essays or stoked by TV news—don't guarantee us anything. Fervent pleas can make a case for compassion or cruelty. So can reasoned arguments.

The key issue is not whether feelings matter. (They do.) Or whether they should. (They always will.) The deeper questions about news media revolve around *which* feelings matter—and whose.

When the focus is on tragic events, media accounts seem to zigzag between pallid facts and easy sentimentality.

Michael Herr, a journalist who covered the Vietnam War, later wrote that the U.S. media "never found a way to report meaningfully about death, which of course was really what it was all about." Obscured by countless news stories, "the suffering was somehow unimpressive."

The same media outlets that can go into paroxysms of grief over one celebrity's demise have shown themselves fully capable of ignoring—or even celebrating—the deaths of many people.

In 1991, when U.S. bombs killed "enemy" soldiers and civilians, the American news media rejoiced. At the end of the slaughter known as the Gulf War, the Pentagon quietly estimated that 200,000 Iraqi people had died as a result of America's firepower. Not a faint breeze of concern blew through U.S. mass media.

Dan Rather—who was to join with other TV news anchors in protracted tribute to Princess Diana a half-dozen years later—went on CBS at the close of February 1991 to warmly shake the hand of a U.S. general and declare: "Congratulations on a job wonderfully done!" On highbrow NPR, which seemed to stand for "National Pentagon Radio" during the war, the enthusiasm for the killing was similarly palpable.

As the fall of 1997 gets underway, a backlash is coming from big-name pundits who bemoan the media response to Diana's death. The glossy news weeklies have had the best of both worlds, pumping up the media furor over her death and then decrying it.

In *Newsweek*'s Sept. 15 issue, George Will denounced the media coverage as "a spectacle both empty and degrading." He lamented that "we have mass media with wondrous capacities for subtracting from understanding by adding to the public's inclination for self-deception and autointoxication."

Will continued: "By turning everyone everywhere into bystanders at events, and by eliciting and amplifying their 'feelings,' the media turn the world into an echo chamber and establish for the promptable masses the appropriate 'reaction' to events."

A week later, with like-minded indignation, Charles Krauthammer filled the last page of *Time* with an attack on "the psychic pleasures of mass frenzy and wallow." He complained: "The public's surrender of its sensibilities and concerns to mass media was never more evident than during the Diana convulsion."

But none of these pundits—Will or Krauthammer, or for that matter Daniel Schorr—could be heard sounding the alarm when media hysteria ignited "patriotic" passion in early 1991. On the contrary, by the time the first missile barrage hit Baghdad, they were among the many journalists pounding the war drums and screaming for blood.

Joseph Stalin would have understood. "The death of one man is a tragedy," he reportedly said at Potsdam in 1945. "The death of millions is a statistic."

Journalists have a responsibility to disprove Stalin's horrible quip. That would require going beyond comfortable biases and striving to treat all human life as precious.

Dylan Thomas, the poetic prince of Wales, advised us to "Rage, rage against the dying of the light." In contrast, all too often, journalism does little more than turn the page.

September 17, 1997

Thirty Years Later,
"A Day in the Life" Resonates

I read the news today, oh boy. About some lucky men and women who made the grade.

A recent issue of *Time* magazine—revealing "The Most Influential People in America"—arrived on newsstands exactly thirty years after the Beatles finished recording their most famous album. That coincidence is worth pondering.

The final surreal song on *Sgt. Pepper's Lonely Hearts Club Band* mounted quite a polemical assault on mainstream news. "A Day in the Life" deftly blasted shallow media fixations.

News media, of course, have gained much more leverage since the day in April 1967 when the Beatles called it a wrap at their Abbey Road studios. Three decades later, the enormous clout of standard media deserves re-examination.

Time's cover story is as good a place as any to start.

Like most artifice designed to capture the public's non-imagination, the magazine's "Most Influential People" gambit needs to drag us over the threshold of customary illusions before it can sink its fangs into our brains.

Our first reaction might be: "What a stupid concept! They can't be serious!" Our next thought will probably be to realize that they are. Moments later, we're reading, and the hook is set. Pretty soon, it's all apt to seem fairly reasonable.

Flipping through the April 21 [1997] edition of *Time*, even before you get to the main story, some powerful messages are hard to miss. The first advertising spread, on a pair of pages just inside the cover, compares the Mercedes-Benz logo—favorably—to a peace sign. ("Right behind every powerful icon lies a powerful idea.")

Turn the page, and a blurb describes the cover story: "*Time*'s roster of the most influential people in America... includes a young golfer and an industrial rocker, a Buddhist activist and an Ivy League encyclopedist, a hapless cartoon character and the irrepressible conscience of the U.S. Senate."

In other words: Tiger Woods and Trent Reznor, Robert Thurman and Henry Louis Gates Jr., Dilbert and Sen. John McCain. Five men and a comic shtick figure. Influential? Maybe. But in this case, more to the point, they're filler between all the slick ads.

There are two-page plugs for Microsoft, sporty Ford trucks, a Chrysler luxury car ("Are you keeping up?"), a deluxe Jeep ("Four Wheeler of the Year"), an antacid to control heartburn, a medical-insurance plan, a Lexus coupe ("now priced from $39,495") and Sun Microsystems—all before the start of the color-splashed pageantry about *Time*'s 25 Most Influential Americans."

Who made the grade? "People whose styles are imitated," the magazine explains, "whose ideas are adopted and whose examples are followed."

Passive voice comes in handy here, allowing *Time* to get the idea across without quite rubbing our noses in it: Who is presumably doing the imitating, adopting and following? You and me. The United Sheep of America.

Those supposedly in the saddle, rounding us up and herding us along, include the editor of the *National Enquirer*, radio shock-jock Don Imus, TV talk-show host Rosie O'Donnell, Colin Powell, Madeleine Albright, a fashion designer, two musicians and an inevitable "web entrepreneur."

To add a bit more realism, the magazine also lists a couple of very wealthy men with divergent politics, Richard Scaife and George Soros—plus Treasury Secretary Robert Rubin, who just happens to be "a centimillionaire." Out of the twenty-five visionary sheepherders, Rubin actually has the closest proximity to the nation's power centers.

But such a listing of "The Most Influential People" winds up inviting us to mire ourselves in the vicarious images of personalities. The spotlight falls without context.

"A Day in the Life" evokes the vast distances between routine media preoccupations and what we experience on a daily basis as we go about our lives. Mostly, the mass media offer white noise and trivia instead of depth and meaning.

"And though the holes were rather small / They had to count them all."

April 16, 1997

Part XII
Worshipping Media Heroes, Old and New

Letting Media Myths Rest in Peace

Back in the early '60s, Alan Shepard and Robert Young cast huge shadows on the national media stage. So, after the heroic astronaut and the famous actor both died on the night of July 21 [1998], the media coverage stirred up memories that are dim yet deep.

On May 5, 1961, when Shepard became the first American to fly into space, he electrified the nation. In those days, we were hearing a lot about a torch that had been passed to a new generation. Shepard served as a symbol of youthful vigor and high-tech prowess.

The media emphasis was on technological achievement fused with cold-warrior firmness. The best and the brightest macho men would bear any burden, pay any price for democracy. Rhetoric about a New Frontier implied renewal of America's pioneer roots. Like the Indians who had perished in past centuries, the poor of the Third World were beside the point.

It seemed fitting that Shepard's brief and historic flight was in a space capsule dubbed "Freedom 7." Shepard and the six other Mercury astronauts were America's A-team in the space race. President Kennedy declared—prophetically—that the United States could land a man on the moon by the end of the decade.

In the media spirit of the times, NASA epitomized the nation's strong sense of purpose. But such steely resolve never developed to pursue goals like ending poverty in this country, or seeing to it that all children could grow up with equal access to the resources of society.

Meanwhile, as front pages told of America's breakthroughs in space, the most popular TV entertainment included *Father Knows Best*. The program had an endearing quality. Mild humor and kindness prevailed. Minor tensions created just enough turmoil to make the televised drama seem plausible.

On *Father Knows Best*, Robert Young was good-natured and reassuring, week after week and year after year. The show remained on prime-time national television from 1954 to 1963. But off camera, in his own life, the man playing the father who knew best was struggling with alcoholism. "I drank, and I drank a lot," he later recalled.

Outwardly confident—even serene—on the set, Young was inwardly consumed with fright. "For over thirty years," he was to remember, "I lived almost every waking hour filled with fear. Fear of many things—the unknown—of some expected calamity around the corner that never comes. A feeling that this stardom I was lucky enough to attain would not last, that I was not worthy, that I didn't deserve it."

But when we watched *Father Knows Best*, we were apt to measure ourselves against the mythic characters—the parents, Margaret and Jim Anderson, and their kids named Betty ("Princess"), Bud and Kathy ("Kitten"). For them, doubts and confusion seemed slight.

Looking back on *Father Knows Best*, seventeen years after the shooting stopped, the actor who'd played Bud gave voice to the kind of introspection that was anathema to the program. "I'm ashamed I had any part of it," Billy Gray said. "People felt warmly about the show and that show did everybody a disservice."

Gray perceived that he'd had a role in a deceptive project: "I felt that the show purported to be real life, and it wasn't. I regret that it was ever presented as a model to live by." One of the biggest drawbacks had to do with rigid gender stereotypes that the program taught and reinforced. "The show contributed a lot to the problems between men and women that we see today."

Styles have changed, but today's media products are still fabrications. To a great extent, the larger-than-life images that take up residence on TV screens and glossy magazine covers—and in our minds—are designed and manufactured as surely as Beanie Babies and new cars. Their value and meaning are vastly overrated.

The guy who played Bud for all those years on *Father Knows Best* went on to offer some cautionary words about media heroes: "I think we were all well motivated but what we did was run a hoax. We weren't trying to, but that is what it was. Just a hoax."

July 22, 1998

Time Magazine's Skewed Tribute to Henry Luce

The nation's biggest news weekly is celebrating itself. *Time* magazine has put out a "75th Anniversary Issue," paying tribute to the vision of founder Henry Luce. Readers get an inspiring—and expurgated—story.

Time began as a pathbreaking newsmagazine in March 1923, the special edition recalls, and Luce was "its undisputed leader for nearly forty years." We're told that he wanted *Time* to be "a vehicle of moral and political instruction, a point of connection between the world of elite ideas and opinion and middle-class people in the 'true' America hungry for knowledge."

Luce died in 1967, and the magazine is now the flagship of the largest media conglomerate ever, Time Warner. But the firm still doffs its corporate hat to the Luce mythology. After more than sixty pages devoted to self-homage, *Time* closes its March 9 [1998] issue with an essay by managing editor Walter Isaacson that clings to the Luce mantle.

While acknowledging that Luce let his "global agendas" unduly influence *Time*'s content, Isaacson assures us that the rough edges have been smoothed: "Although our stories often have a strong point of view, we try to make sure they are informed by open-minded reporting rather than partisan biases." Yet the magazine lays claim to Luce's core values: "Above all, we continue to share his belief that journalism can be, at its best, a noble endeavor."

But *Time*'s 75th anniversary issue is a telling instance of how lofty rhetoric can easily serve as a cover story. The hero of the retrospective, Henry Luce, gets plenty of adulation and some hazy references to flaws. But it's sanitized history, omitting less pleasant facts.

They aren't hard to find. As tragic events unfolded in Europe, Luce ran his thriving magazine empire with an odious tilt. "In 1934 he devoted an entire issue of *Fortune* to glorifying

Mussolini and Fascism," wrote independent journalist George Seldes. And in *Time*, Luce "permitted an outright pro-fascist, Laird Goldsborough, to slant and pervert the news every week."

In the mid-1930s, Luce often expressed admiration for the far-right advances in Europe. "The moral force of Fascism, appearing in totally different forms in different nations, may be the inspiration for the next general march of mankind," he told one audience.

Meanwhile, *Time* played a pivotal role. Luce biographer W.A. Swanberg documents that "when the lights of liberty were going out and the forces of brutality and oppression were rising, *Time* was guilty of throwing its considerable weight in favor of Mussolini and Hitler."

When Nazi forces remilitarized the Rhineland in 1936, *Time's* reporting "took a sentimental view," Swanberg writes in *Luce and His Empire*—"quite as if it were a joyous festival instead of a grave step toward war." And when Hitler "coolly announced another treaty breach in the secret Nazi organization of an air force equal to England's, *Time* described it with great good humor as 'Hitler's exit from the jam closet, sticky-faced,' and said, 'Germany has been naughty but is not to be spanked.' "

Late in the decade, *Time* began to denounce Hitler and Mussolini, with detailed coverage of their evil deeds. "Had not *Time* for so long applauded the Fascist dictators," Swanberg comments, "these things would not so badly have needed saying."

One of many brilliant books by Seldes, *Witness to a Century*, recounts a revealing incident in March 1942: "Thurman Arnold, the assistant attorney general, appearing before a Senate committee investigating war profiteering, testified that Ethyl Gasoline Corporation, General Motors, Standard Oil and I.G. Farben of Germany had an agreement by which the American corporations supplied Hitler with the secret of making tetra-ethyl lead for gasoline, without which Hitler could not have operated his air force or gone to war, and also supplied him with the secrets of making synthetic rubber."

The head of the committee, Sen. Harry Truman, responded by declaring "This is treason." But the big press glossed over the matter. As Seldes noted: "Henry Luce's *Time*, for example, ridiculed Truman on page 16 one week and published a $5,000 Standard Oil advertisement on page 89."

After formation of the Central Intelligence Agency in 1947, Luce—a close friend of U.S. spymaster Allen Dulles—privately urged his correspondents to cooperate with the agency. Meanwhile, Luce debriefed with the CIA about his own travels overseas.

Along with some other powerful media executives, Luce joined Dulles on the board of directors of the National Committee for a Free Europe. That private front group funneled money to neo-Nazi émigré organizations.

Fifty-seven years ago, Luce proclaimed that the world was in the midst of "The American Century." His pronouncement is still echoing.

On March 3, when *Time* spent $3 million to throw a celebrity-filled anniversary party at Radio City Music Hall in New York, one of the featured guests was Bill Clinton. "Tonight, *Time* magazine has paid tribute to the time it not only observed but helped to shape," the president said, "the 100 stunning years that your founder Henry Luce so unforgettably called the American Century."

Time Warner bigwigs like the sound of such talk. And they see no reason for the United States to relinquish the next hundred years. "To the extent that America remains an avatar of freedom," *Time*'s managing editor contends, "the Global Century about to dawn will be, in Luce's terminology, another American Century."

No thanks. One was more than enough.

March 4, 1998

M. WUERKER

The New Media Heroes: "Corporate Rebels"

By now, we've run across similar stories many times: A scrappy innovator took on the business establishment and made a fortune. An engineer battled myopic bosses to develop a great new product. A brilliant computer nerd overcame entrenched foes and now heads the firm.

Today's news reports seem to be more focused on mutiny than conformity in corporate suites. At a time when many companies are urging employees to challenge old concepts, the media coverage often makes the latest changes sound almost radical.

Nowhere is this media tone more fervent than at *Wired* magazine. Founded in 1993, the colorful monthly calls itself the journal of "the Digital Revolution"—and honors its readers as "digital revolutionaries."

Wired went over the 300,000 circulation mark in early 1996. The ornate magazine is quite influential with an affluent readership—including many journalists—eager to keep tabs on cutting-edge computer trends.

When *Wired* published a special twelve-page report titled "Corporate Rebels" (May 1997), it cranked up the rhetoric of revolt. "Inflexible bureaucracy, top-down management, tightly regulated industries, monopoly—these are the tired remnants of the old corporate world order," *Wired* proclaimed in big type.

But the magazine saw hope: "Those who break the shackles of business as usual—corporate rebels—set the pace for the next millennium. They are iconoclasts who question the status quo, cut through red tape, and challenge their bosses to greatness… The smarter companies tap the uprising within, creating ways to turn the steam of the rebel into the fuel that drives the business."

That's the kind of muddled verbiage that provides a hospitable environment for sleek full-page ads from outfits like

Intel, Sony, Lucent Technologies, Microsoft, Panasonic and U.S. Robotics.

Wired mingles technical updates and human-interest features with idolatry of huge corporations now gaining unprecedented control over systems of mass communication. Evidently, *Wired*'s editors are complacent about the dire implications for democracy.

In recent years, *Time* and *Newsweek* have imitated a bit of *Wired*'s style. But while the news weeklies can print only a few cyber-fixated pages, *Wired* pumps out more than 200 in a single issue.

And the hero worship is remarkable.

For instance, IBM research fellow Ted Selker—*Wired*'s leading Corporate Rebel—earned the headline "Rebel Without a Pause." *Wired* explained that Selker had a cause: He "battled engineering and manufacturing skeptics to create the track-point, the knobby red pointing device that helped boost sales of IBM's ThinkPad portable PC."

Wow! That's a rebel for you.

Right behind him were other *Wired* heroes: the wealthy founder of a discount global phone service; the designer of "a radical companywide internal network" for U S West Communications; a pioneer of online stock brokering...

Wired's pretenses are grimly laughable. The magazine glorifies a procession of vaunted rebels for struggling to persuade a corporate hierarchy to let them generate profits. In a vague echo of '60s counterculture and New Age platitudes, these crusades are likened to the sacred quest for human freedom.

The limits aren't hard to discern. When the magazine's corporate parent, Wired Ventures, tried to attract investment capital in 1996, it boasted that "none of the company's employees is represented by a labor union." Today, with more than 300 people on the Wired Ventures payroll, that's still the case.

While *Wired* praises pseudo-rebels for "challenging conventional wisdom," the proof of their virtue is a higher rate of return. Rebellion is laudable if it results in making more money for the company.

Of course, according to some mainstream news outlets, *Wired* itself qualifies as a corporate rebel. The *New York Times* has dubbed *Wired* "the icon of the Internet generation." The newspaper declared: "The genius of *Wired* is that it makes the Digital Revolution a self-fulfilling prophesy, both illuminating this new sub-culture and promoting it."

Despite all the hype, skilled technicians and shrewd investors don't merit acclaim as profound visionaries.

"Happy is the country which requires no heroes," said the German playwright Bertolt Brecht. Such a nation may not exist today. But at least we might hope for a country where the news media can tell the difference between a heroic rebel and a clever entrepreneur.

June 11, 1997

Katharine Graham's Post

When Katharine Graham's memoirs appeared in early 1997, the media accolades were profuse. "Extraordinary," wrote *New York Times* reviewer Christopher Lehmann-Haupt. "You chew your nails down to the nub for her... That she grew and finally succeeded is inspiring." In the Sunday *Times*, Nora Ephron praised *Personal History* as a "riveting, moving auto-biography"—"wonderful" and brimming with "candor and forthrightness." NPR's *All Things Considered* and *Fresh Air* featured long and reverential interviews with the author. Even *Time* magazine, assessing the book by the owner of archrival *Newsweek*, called it "disarmingly candid."

A huge bestseller, *Personal History* is well on its way to status as a classic. Typically, syndicated columnist Mary McGrory lauded "a drop-dead honest story of a woman who tremblingly took over the management of the *Washington Post* after her brilliant husband's suicide—and changed the face of American journalism." McGrory, who is based at the *Post*, speculated that the book will soon be required reading for high school students.

Readers glimpse some of Katharine Graham's most painful memories: her bittersweet upbringing with distant parents; sorrows that came with early adulthood, including the loss of her first child at birth; the descent of her husband Philip Graham into years of manic-depression that ended when he killed himself with a shotgun in 1963. As Kay Graham recounts a lifelong quest to overcome routine sexism, her efforts to gain self-esteem and confidence provide a crucial narrative thread.

Personal History is also a very political yarn about journalism—but few enthusiasts have scrutinized the book in those terms. Enthralled with her hard-earned evolution from downtrodden female to powerful businesswoman, reviewers and interviewers accepted as a given the high quality and integrity of the journalistic enterprise she ran: the Washington Post Company.

"I don't believe that whom I was or wasn't friends with interfered with our reporting at any of our publications," Graham writes. However, Robert Parry—who was a Washington correspondent for *Newsweek* during the last three years of the 1980s—can shed some light on the shadows of Graham's reassuring prose. Parry told me that he witnessed "self-censorship because of the coziness between *Post-Newsweek* executives and senior national security figures."

Among Parry's examples: "On one occasion in 1987, I was told that my story about the CIA funneling anti-Sandinista money through Nicaragua's Catholic Church had been watered down because the story needed to be run past Mrs. Graham, and Henry Kissinger was her house guest that weekend. Apparently, there was fear among the top editors that the story as written might cause some consternation." (The 1996 memoirs of former CIA Director Robert Gates confirmed that Parry had it right all along.)

Graham's book exudes affection for Kissinger as well as Robert McNamara, George Shultz and other Cabinet luminaries who have remained dear friends. Likewise, many business titans are rendered as near-saints. Graham intimate Warren Buffett—a major stockholder and boardmember of the Washington Post Company—is served up as a blend of Mister Greenjeans and Albert Einstein, with impish zest for acquiring billions. Buffett's interests are singular, she explains with admiration: "What he loves is business—thinking and reading and talking about business." What comes through clearly is her worship of Buffett, a corporate raider now ranked as the country's second-richest man. (The *Post*'s coverage of Buffett has been effusive. "He burps and he's in the newspaper," says Ralph Nader.)

"When I look back over my long life," reflects the famous daughter of Wall Street tycoon Eugene Meyer, who bought the *Washington Post* in 1933, "if there is one thing that leaps out at me it is the role of luck and chance in our lives." Yet Katharine Graham expresses great pleasure at the momentum of her media firm as it moves further from concern about the less fortunate.

Hostility toward young black people mired in poverty has become thematic at the *Post*—and *Newsweek*. For years the magazine vented the outbursts of staffer Joe Klein, who was repeating himself when he wrote in 1993 that "out-of-wedlock births to teenagers are at the heart of the nexus of pathologies that define the underclass." Colleagues learned to harmonize. Jonathan Alter (a "stellar" journalist in Graham's book) proclaimed the next year, "The fact remains: every threat to the fabric of this country—from poverty to crime to homelessness—is connected to out-of-wedlock teen pregnancy."

In retrospect, a quarter of a century ago there was much symbolism in the *Post*'s embrace of George Will, who chose to become a syndicated *Post* columnist rather than continue as a speechwriter for Jesse Helms. Today, Will—who also graces *Newsweek*—has plenty of ideological companionship on the *Post*'s op-ed page, where veteran rightist Robert Novak holds a steady berth alongside newer recruits such as James Glassman, Robert Samuelson and Charles Krauthammer. The dominant debate on the page pits pro-corporate reactionaries against pro-corporate centrists. After the *Post* fired the exceptional columnist Colman McCarthy in late 1996, managing editor Robert Kaiser said that it opted to "take a cue from the marketplace"; the number of papers buying McCarthy's syndicated column had dropped.

At the *Post*, corporatized markets rule. Another straw in the wind was the recent cancellation of Jack Anderson's column, a fixture in the paper since the 1960s; his product was hardly left-wing, but it stepped on enough big-money toes to unsettle management. During the NAFTA debate in 1993, pro-NAFTA sources quoted in the *Post*'s news coverage outnumbered anti-NAFTA sources by 71 percent to 17 percent. Among scores of op-ed page articles, the pro-NAFTA ratio was 6 to 1. Later, during the GATT battle, *Post* editorials pushed hard for approval of the global trade pact, and *Post* publisher Donald Graham personally lobbied Congress and the executive branch. As it happened, the Washington Post Company had millions of dollars at stake with GATT.

Corporate solidarity has led the *Post* to close ranks—in editorials and in federal court—with foes of adequate product liability. In a May 1996 letter to the editor (which the *Post* declined to print), Public Citizen's president Joan Claybrook noted that the Post Company "has filed briefs in the U.S. Supreme Court supporting limits on punitive damages in civil lawsuits, although this fact was not disclosed in the *Post*'s many editorials on the subject."

Members of the *Post* hierarchy are pursuing their financial interests. "They represent the corporate conglomerate that they are," says Ralph Nader. "They have a party line on globalization. They refuse to examine the shibboleth of 'free trade.' " As early as 1989, Nader was contending that "one of the best-kept secrets in journalism is the transformation of the *Washington Post* into a right-wing newspaper." His current appraisal? The *Post* "is becoming more and more corporatist." He condemns "their lack of critical coverage of corporate power in this town... They're very much official-source journalism." The *Post* is "part of the oligarchy."

The *Post* has grown particularly conservative on economic issues, as *The Washington Monthly* showed in November 1995. Writer Amy Waldman documented the corporate slant pervading the paper, including the financial pages—where "much more of the business coverage serves as a press-release-based bulletin board for company profits, mergers, and personnel moves." Meanwhile, consumer reporting has become sporadic; the vigorous reporter on that beat for three decades, Morton Mintz, retired in 1988, and the *Post* has done little to fill the gap.

But it would be a mistake to laud good old days. The *Post*'s entanglements with government policy-makers go back a long way. Publisher Phil Graham, a frenetic power-broker who aided his buddies Lyndon Johnson and John Kennedy, maintained warm friendships with CIA officials. He knew many secrets that he kept out of the *Post*, such as plans for the 1961 Bay of Pigs invasion. Styles have changed since then, but the Post Company has preserved strong bonds with Washington's movers and shakers.

Unmentioned in Katharine Graham's lengthy book is the Gulf of Tonkin incident in early August 1964. She had been president of the Washington Post Company for almost a year by then. Considering the consequences of the congressional Tonkin Gulf resolution that followed days later, the *Post*'s coverage—which presented falsehoods as absolute facts—might have merited a few words.

But Graham's book avoids any semblance of introspection about the Vietnam War and the human costs of her craven behavior. In August 1966 she huddled with a writer in line to take charge of the editorial page: "We agreed that the *Post* ought to work its way out of the very supportive editorial position it had taken, but that we couldn't be precipitous; we had to move away gradually from where we had been." Many years of carnage resulted from such unwillingness to "be precipitous."

Graham's passions, personal and political, run elsewhere: "Some of my deepest friendships began with an administration person whom I got to know because of my association with the paper—Bob McNamara and Henry Kissinger come immediately to mind—but grew over time into relationships whose core had nothing to do with politics or work." While those ties grew, others frayed.

Joe Rauh, a liberal strategist and old friend, was no stranger to dubious compromises. But during the 1980s he recoiled as the *Post* cozied up to the Reagan administration. When the paper endorsed Edwin Meese for confirmation as attorney general (with a regulatory quid pro quo a real possibility for the Post Company), Rauh submitted a contrary op-ed piece to the newspaper. After rejection, Rauh went to an editorial-board meeting but got nowhere. In an interview with Katharine Graham biographer Carol Felsenthal, Rauh recalled what her son Donald Graham had said as they walked to a taxi outside the *Post* building: "Mr. Rauh, you have to remember one thing: This is not the liberal paper that you remember."

Acknowledging none of this in her book, Kay Graham skips over the *Post*'s rightward direction. That's appropriate, since the company line remains denial. When, this year, I asked managing editor Kaiser about the *Post*'s move to the right, he insisted that it had never occurred.

Katharine Graham is truly a bipartisan spirit. She recalls that two of her maids watched a limousine pull up when Ronald Reagan came over for dinner soon after winning the presidency: "They saw President-elect Reagan step out and embrace me, kissing me on both cheeks." During the 1980s, she and Nancy Reagan became pals, their lunches often joined by *Post* editorial-page editor Meg Greenfield. In December 1992, Graham threw a dinner party for President-elect Bill Clinton and Al Gore. As the guests of honor beamed, Graham raised her glass in a toast. "These occasions have value," she declared. "They create relationships beyond the office."

For Graham, those relationships entail special burdens. "There have been instances," she stated years ago, "in which secrets have been leaked to us which we thought were so dangerous that we went to them [U.S. officials] and told them that they had been leaked to us and did not print them." In November 1988, speaking to senior CIA officials at the agency headquarters in Langley, Virginia, she said: "There are some things the general public does not need to know and shouldn't. I believe democracy flourishes when the government can take legitimate steps to keep its secrets and when the press can decide whether to print what it knows."

Highly image-conscious, *Personal History* has no use for that kind of talk. But the book devotes dozens of righteous pages to the pivotal 1975 strike by *Post* press operators. Graham stresses the damage done to printing equipment as the walk-out began and "the unforgivable acts of violence throughout the strike." It is a profound commentary on her outlook that thuggish deeds by a few of the strikers were "unforgivable"—while men like McNamara and Kissinger were lovable after they oversaw horrendous slaughter in Southeast Asia.

The strike ended with permanent "replacement workers" hired, the pressmen's union broken and management in command of labor relations at the *Post*. (The weakened Newspaper Guild is still paying for its failure to stay out in support of the pressmen.) During the several months of the strike, the *Post* actually turned a profit. But the real yields for management were yet to come. "Without the groundwork laid by the strike, we would not have been able to build and to grow," Graham crows. And she reports: "Even those publishers who denounced the so-called liberalism of the *Post*'s news and editorial pages applauded our actions on the management side."

Graham portrays union stalwarts as mostly ruffians or dupes. "Only a handful of guild members had gone out for reasons I respected," she tells readers. "One was John Hanrahan, a good reporter and a nice man who came from a longtime labor family and simply couldn't cross a picket line. He never did come back. Living your beliefs is a rare virtue and greatly to be admired." But for Hanrahan (whose Republican parents actually never belonged to a union) the admiration is far from mutual. In his words: "The *Washington Post* under Katharine Graham pioneered the union-busting 'replacement worker' strategy that Ronald Reagan subsequently used against the air-traffic controllers and that corporate America—in the Caterpillar, Bridgestone/Firestone and other strikes—used to throw thousands of workers out of their jobs in the 1980s and the '90s."

The Washington Post Company came of age as a major corporation during the 1970s. Early in the decade it went public under an arrangement that allowed the Grahams, as "A" class stockholders, to retain control of the firm. Going on the American Stock Exchange "gave us some proper discipline about profit margins," Katharine Graham writes, "although I worry about the overemphasis at times on the price of stock."

Graham announced in the mid-'70s that she expected profits of at least 15 percent—and this became, de facto, the Graham family "politics." Now, with eighty years behind her, Katharine

Graham is continuing to loosen her grip on a media empire left to Donald Graham and investors hungry to maximize profits.

Preoccupied with such concerns as "the price of the stock," the company persists in distancing itself from independent journalism. Meanwhile, the *Post*'s role in helping to set the national media agenda is immense. The news it reports and the opinions it showcases have enormous repercussions; so do the everyday refusals to include perspectives that seem irrelevant or threatening to elites.

For a book so widely touted as a feminist parable, *Personal History* is notably bereft of solidarity for women without affluence or white skin. They barely seem to exist in Katharine Graham's range of vision; wrenching realities of class and race are dim, faraway specks. She does not seem inquisitive about why the *Post* has encountered so many formal complaints about racial and gender bias. And Graham's 625 pages make no mention of former *Washington Post* staff writer Jill Nelson—whose book *Volunteer Slavery* is a genuinely blunt account of working in the *Post*'s newsroom between 1986 and 1990. Nelson's grim experiences as a black woman directly contradict Graham's upbeat version of conditions at the paper.

Overall, Graham gives short shrift to the unrich and unfamous, whose background noise is peripheral to the real drama played out by her dazzling peers. Even activists who made history are mere walk-ons. The name of Martin Luther King Jr. does not appear in her star-studded, history-drenched book.

Today, Katharine Graham's priorities find frequent echo in the *Post*'s local preoccupations. When two well-known men died in Washington within ten days of each other this spring [1997], the contrast was revealing. The death of sports magnate Jack Kent Cooke set off massive and adulatory coverage in the *Post*, which splashed dozens of articles eulogizing him as a heroic figure. But the passing of the D.C. Council's longtime chairman David A. Clarke was marked by a few restrained news items. Clarke's decades of grassroots efforts for the poor and dispossessed of the city, and his twelve years as D.C.'s number-two elected official, seemed to count for little. In the judgment holding sway at the *Post*, the life of Cooke—who amassed several hundred million dollars he couldn't take with him—was much more worthy of celebration.

The laudatory media response to Katharine Graham's autobiography testifies to exalted low standards. The *Post* and *Newsweek* represent what legions of journalists and media executives wish to emulate. Her fervent embrace of corporate power is hardly conspicuous; on the contrary, it is an affirmation of shared faith. "I was and am a centrist," Graham writes: a mass-media applause line if ever there was one.

"The greatest triumphs of propaganda have been accomplished, not by doing something, but by refraining from doing," Aldous Huxley observed a half-century ago. "Great is truth, but still greater, from a practical point of view, is silence about truth." Katharine Graham's book is filled with such silence. The mainstream journalists praising her candor didn't seem to notice.

[In April 1998—about ten months after a version of this article appeared in *The Progressive* magazine—Katharine Graham's book *Personal History* won the Pulitzer Prize for autobiography.]

June 1997

Part XIII
Expelling Heretics From
Media Temples

Newspaper's Conscience
Gets Tossed Overboard

You could almost hear the clink of expensive champagne glasses in the nation's capital when the most influential newspaper inside the Beltway published a column under the headline "So Long, With Thanks."

Colman McCarthy, a man known as the conscience of the *Washington Post*, said goodbye to readers [on Jan. 8, 1997] with typical grace and optimism. He did so despite the fact that—after eighteen years as a *Post* columnist—he'd been dumped overboard by media big shots.

A conscience is always in danger of wearing out its welcome. And the 58-year-old McCarthy lacks a record of trimming his sails to suit the prevailing winds.

Although more than two dozen newspapers around the country were still printing McCarthy's column, the Washington Post Writers Group syndicate decided to pull the plug—and the flagship paper opted to do the same. "We agreed that the column had run its course," the *Post*'s managing editor, Robert Kaiser, told me.

It's true that McCarthy is a bit out of fashion. He doesn't search for loopholes in such ancient concepts as "Thou shalt not kill." He writes about nonviolence as a spiritual force. He dares to advocate for the hungry and the homeless. He is preoccupied with compassion as an active principle instead of a passive piety.

In the city of Washington, teeming with hard-boiled calculators, McCarthy earned little fondness from Republican or Democratic officials. While they jockeyed for partisan advantage, he focused on people excluded from the political race entirely.

During the Gulf War, he was virtually alone among the commentators whose newsprint words fell on the doorsteps of armchair warriors. McCarthy has never wavered from the goal of beating swords into plowshares.

Now, the politicians and the generals, the arms contractors and the corporate lobbyists won't have to see McCarthy's column in the august *Washington Post*. No other regular columnist in the newspaper—which unfolds across the breakfast tables of Washington's high and mighty—is nearly as willing to disregard the unspoken taboos.

"What should be the moral purpose of writing," McCarthy asked in his final *Post* column, "if not to embrace ideals that can help fulfill the one possibility we all yearn for, the peaceable society? Peace is the result of love and if love were easy, we'd all be good at it."

He added: "I've sought out the experts at love—the only expertise that matters. In whichever town or neighborhood I went into, unfailingly I could find someone or some group—usually unnoticed—advancing human possibilities. These were citizens of high spiritual voltage, dissenters from safe opinions who tended not to be picked up on the scan of conventional media."

McCarthy remained acutely aware that would-be pundits are only worth much if they forget punditry and strive to illuminate the central concerns of humanity. He rushed to write his column where the slick media angels are too fearful, or too jaded, to tread.

Meanwhile, for many years, McCarthy has been a volunteer teacher at high schools and colleges. He joins with students to pursue a sacred endeavor—not how to get ahead but how to find one's heart in a process of creative nonviolence. His writings have always reflected that quest.

After showing McCarthy the door, *Post* managers are citing a gradual decline in revenue from syndication of his column. "Maybe I should be amazed that I was being printed for twenty-seven years, so in that sense I'm grateful," says McCarthy, who joined the *Post* staff in the late 1960s. "But I can't help feeling puzzled by being ousted over an issue of profitability—especially when profits are high at the paper."

It was appropriate that McCarthy's last column included a challenging quote from Martin Luther King Jr.: "Our only hope today lies in our ability to recapture the revolutionary spirit and go out into a sometimes hostile world declaring eternal hostility to poverty, racism and militarism."

Such talk makes some people uncomfortable—especially when it persists. The *Washington Post*'s top editors, evidently, have run out of patience.

January 8, 1997

A Media Tale About
Three Men and a Mouse

This is a story about three men and a mouse. The men are named Ted, Danny and Jim. The mouse is named Mickey. And the moral of the story is—well, that's for you to decide.

Late last month [October 1997], at the International Press Freedom Awards Dinner in New York, ABC News superstar Ted Koppel received a lifetime achievement prize. In a brief speech, he lamented the "fading lines between television news and entertainment." And he warned that American journalists are threatened by "the trivialization of our industry."

Decrying the sorry state of America's airwaves has become a ritual among the most famous names in broadcast news—who step away from their multimillion-dollar jobs just long enough to tell us how concerned they are about the mess they're still helping to perpetuate.

Perhaps Koppel should take a serious look at *The More You Watch, the Less You Know*, a new book by Danny Schechter—published, coincidentally, the day before Koppel delivered his high-sounding speech.

After eight years as a producer at ABC's *20/20* program, Schechter left the network in 1988 and proceeded to find meaningful work—by creating it. Since then, his output with like-minded colleagues has included documentaries ranging from South Africa to Bosnia. He also co-produced *Rights & Wrongs: Human Rights Television*, a regular series that aired on public TV from 1993 to 1996 (without support from PBS).

Schechter's feisty new book is not an attempt to compensate for daily conformity. Instead, it's an extension of gutsy endeavors that have typified his work as a media insider and outsider.

The biases of network television don't amount to a conspiracy, he explains: "No, rarely is someone picking up the phone and telling some producer to skew the news. The boardroom rarely faxes orders to the newsroom. But then again, they don't have to if they hire professionals who share the same worldview and language, rely on the same sources, and tend to shape their reporting the same way."

In spite of the sad media saga he recounts, Schechter exudes optimism. "It doesn't have to be this way," he contends early in the book. Nearly 400 pages later, he insists: "When the public understands the issues and takes up the challenge, change can happen, despite all of the media's arrogance and seductive power."

Schechter adds: "Fighting to democratize the media will not be an easy or quick fight, and cannot be won before the next commercial break. Eternal vigilance is still what's needed."

A week after *The More You Watch, the Less You Know* appeared, another excellent book by a former ABC employee was published. The author: Jim Hightower. The title: *There's Nothing in the Middle of the Road But Yellow Stripes and Dead Armadillos*.

Since working as the Texas agriculture commissioner during the 1980s, Hightower has immersed himself in creating media of, by and for the people. He has a whale of a tale to tell—and he tells it with deft analysis and wit.

Hightower describes how his stint as a national radio host for ABC came to an end in 1995. "My ABC weekend show had been airing for about a year," he recalls, "blasting the powers-that-be and preaching the populist gospel, when Disney Inc. announced on Tuesday, Aug. 1, that it was buying my network. Suddenly I was the property of Mickey Mouse."

When his program began the following Saturday, Hightower announced: "I work for a rodent." He went on to denounce the Disney takeover as well as the Telecommunications Act that had just passed the Senate, paving the way for accelerated media mergers and buyouts.

"Turns out the mouse doesn't have much of a sense of humor," Hightower writes, "and there was an abrupt chilling in the network's enthusiasm for my program. Even though ABC had until then been committed to the steady growth of the show…and even though there were numerous advertisers available to back the show—I was suddenly moused, literally kicked off the air shortly after my anti-Mickey, anti-merger broadcast."

Looking ahead, Mickey's parent company will probably remain inhospitable to journalists like Danny Schechter and commentators like Jim Hightower. As one of the biggest media conglomerates, Disney is scurrying to the beat of a very loud corporate drum. And that beat goes on. Just ask Ted Koppel.

November 5, 1997

Ignored Oscar Film
Sets Inspiring Example

George Seldes would have chuckled at the media silence that greeted the Oscar nomination for a movie about him.

Few modern journalists are aware of the greatest press critic in this nation's history. So, it's not surprising that most media outlets have ignored *Tell the Truth and Run: George Seldes and the American Press.*

In contrast, another 1997 Academy Award finalist for best documentary feature—*When We Were Kings*, a film about Muhammad Ali's boxing comeback in 1974—has gotten lots of publicity. It's owned by Gramercy Pictures, part of the huge Polygram conglomerate.

The documentary about Seldes did not receive any corporate backing. The film's producer and director, Rick Goldsmith, created *Tell the Truth and Run* in much the same way that Seldes lived his life: independently.

"The most sacred cow of the press is the press itself," Seldes concluded. Early in his journalistic career, he learned just how harmful media self-worship could be.

When Armistice Day brought World War I to an end, Seldes broke ranks with the obedient press corps and drove behind the lines of retreating German troops. For the rest of his life, Seldes remained haunted by what took place next.

Seldes and three colleagues secured an interview with Paul von Hindenburg, the German field marshal. Seldes asked what had ended the war. "The American infantry in the Argonne won the war," Hindenburg responded, and elaborated before breaking into sobs.

It was an enormous scoop. But allied military censors blocked Hindenburg's admission, which he never repeated in public.

The story could have seriously undermined later Nazi claims that Germany had lost the war due to a "stab in the back" by Jews and leftists. Seldes came to believe that the inter-view, if published, "would have destroyed the main planks of the platform on which Hitler rose to power." But the reporters involved "did not think it worthwhile to give up our number-one positions in journalism" by disobeying military censors "in order to be free to publish."

Seldes gathered firsthand news about many historic fig-ures. Lenin did not appreciate the young American journalist, and neither did Mussolini. The Bolsheviks banished Seldes from the Soviet Union in 1923. Two years later, with Black Shirt thugs on his heels, Seldes caught a train out of Italy.

In 1928, after nearly ten years as a foreign correspondent for the *Chicago Tribune*, Seldes quit—fed up with biased editing. The last straw came with the newspaper's selective use of his dispatches from Mexico. Articles presenting the perspective of U.S. oil companies promptly ran in full, but stories about the contrary views of the Mexican government did not.

Seldes became a trailblazing press critic. Starting in 1929, he wrote intrepid books—such as *You Can't Print That* and *Lords of the Press*—endearing him to readers but infuriating media moguls of the day. Seldes served as a Diogenes whose light led the way for new generations of journalists eager to search for truth wherever it might lead.

Many of his stands, lonely at the time, were prophetic. Beginning in the late 1930s, for example, Seldes excoriated the American press for hiding the known dangers of smoking while making millions from cigarette ads. He was several decades ahead of his time.

An implacable foe of tyranny, Seldes was not content to cast stones at faraway despots. He also took on mighty centers of power—"big money and big business"—close to home.

Like few other journalists, Seldes shined a fierce light on Europe's emerging fascism—and its allies in the United States. Seldes repeatedly attacked press barons such as William Randolph Hearst and groups like the National Association of Manufacturers for assisting Hitler, Mussolini and Spain's General Francisco Franco.

George Seldes and his wife, Helen, covered the war between Franco's fascists and the coalition of loyalists fighting for the elected Spanish government. A chain of East Coast daily newspapers carried the pair's front-line dispatches—until pressure from U.S. supporters of Franco caused the chain to drop their reports.

From 1940 to 1950, Seldes edited America's first periodical of media criticism. The weekly newsletter, *In fact*, peaked at a circulation of 176,000 copies as it scrutinized the press—"the most powerful force against the general welfare of the majority of the people."

What happened to *In fact*? The *New York Times* obituary about Seldes simply stated that it "ceased publication in 1950, when his warnings about Fascism seemed out of tune with rising public concern about Communism." In fact, however, *In fact* fell victim to an official vendetta.

One FBI tactic was to intimidate readers by having agents in numerous post offices compile the names of *In fact* subscribers. Such harassment was pivotal to the newsletter's demise. Also crucial was the sustained barrage of smears and Red-baiting against *In fact* in the country's largest newspapers.

Seldes was an astute analyst of self-censorship. Most reporters, he observed, "know from contact with the great minds of the press lords or from the simple deduction that the bosses are in big business and the news must be slanted accordingly, or from the general intangible atmosphere which prevails everywhere, what they can do and what they must never do."

Thus, Seldes added, "The most stupid boast in the history of present-day journalism is that of the writer who says, 'I have never been given orders; I am free to do as I like.'"

Today, on my desk is a copy of Seldes' sparkling autobiography, *Witness to a Century*. On the first page, in the graceful handwriting of a 97-year-old man, is an inscription dated May 9, 1988. I treasure the memory of visiting Seldes. And I vividly remember the warm gleam in his eyes as he stood waving goodbye from his porch.

The death of George Seldes—on July 2, 1995, at the age of 104—underscored the major media's lack of interest in legacies of journalistic courage. *Time* magazine devoted forty words to his passing; *Newsweek* didn't mention it at all.

Tell the Truth and Run could win an Academy Award. It's a long shot. But filmmaker Rick Goldsmith has already achieved a great deal with a stirring documentary that preserves the voice and spirit of George Seldes.

Eight days after the announcement of Oscar nominees, I went to the tiny office in Berkeley, California, where Goldsmith has worked on the Seldes movie project since the start of this decade. "The challenge is to find the venues to get the film out to viewers," he said.

Goldsmith's film still lacks distribution to theaters. And the key TV network for documentaries—the PBS system—has so far rebuffed *Tell the Truth and Run*. However, Goldsmith continues to persevere.

Unlike the "independent" movies with piles of money behind them for promotion and distribution, Goldsmith's truly independent documentary remains a celluloid vision on a frayed shoestring. The obstacles have always been formidable. But *Tell the Truth and Run* is a precious film that implores us to think for ourselves—and to fight against all types of media censorship.

[*Tell the Truth and Run* did not win the Academy Award for best documentary feature. The Oscar went to *When We Were Kings*.]

February 19, 1997

Part XIV
Shilling for Profitable Hypocrisy

Nuclear Testing Story
Has Some Big Holes

The Bomb—nearly forgotten by many of us—returned to the world's center stage in a hurry. When India set off several nuclear explosions and President Clinton quickly responded with economic sanctions [in May 1998], the news coverage was jolting.

Condemnation of India's nuclear tests is certainly justified. But the story we're getting is quite partial. The plot narrated by the White House and echoed by the American media—presenting the U.S. government as a principled foe of nuclear escalation—is akin to a fairy tale.

This country's journalists don't have to visit India in order to find alarming evidence of a nuclear arms race. They could venture much closer to home.

Forty miles from San Francisco, scientists at the Lawrence Livermore Laboratory are still designing thermonuclear bombs. Under a benign-sounding Stockpile Stewardship and Management program, the Department of Energy carries on with the business of devising new and "improved" nuclear warheads.

In fact, the U.S. government is spending $4 billion a year to develop nuclear weapons. The effort includes sophisticated computer simulation that enables the United States to upgrade the deadly capabilities of its nuclear arsenal without resorting to test detonations.

Now, more than ever, the Clinton administration is a fount of piety as the president and his top aides scold the transgressors in New Delhi. While lecturing India to show restraint, the U.S. officials continue to lead the world in building a nuclear bridge to the 21st century.

The news media hardly seemed to notice as the United States completed the testing and deployment of B61-11 earth-penetrating nuclear warheads in 1997. And when conflicts with Baghdad intensified over the next winter, we heard little about

Washington's not-so-veiled threat to use such weaponry against Iraq.

Since then, Clinton has overseen a major overhaul of nuclear-weapons policies. And he issued a presidential directive allowing the Pentagon to plan for the use of U.S. atomic weapons against non-nuclear states. Clinton's order violated the Nuclear Non-Proliferation Treaty—the same pact, ironically, that the president cited in reverential tones on May 13 [1998] when he announced sanctions against India.

In February [1998], with a U.S.-Iraq confrontation heating up, Boris Yeltsin warned that "Clinton's actions could lead to a world war." American news media attributed the Russian president's comment to irrational inebriation. The *Los Angeles Times*, for instance, called the remark "somewhat daffy." But Yeltsin was apparently referring to the fact that Clinton had authorized the U.S. military to target Iraq with nuclear arms.

Jay Truman knows quite a bit about nuclear tests. Growing up in southern Utah during the 1950s, he watched mushroom clouds rise from the Nevada Test Site about 110 miles to the west. While in high school, Truman was diagnosed with lymphoma. Unlike many of his classmates, he survived.

Now, Truman is director of a regional organization known as Downwinders. "There is no excuse or justification for any nuclear weapons testing by any nation," he told me. "But before everyone starts pointing their fingers at India as the world's only nuclear villain, it's important to look at the ongoing weapons development programs of the United States and the other members of the 'perm five'—the established nuclear weapons countries—and clean up our own houses first."

Truman emphasizes that "the nuclear arms race will not be over until all nuclear weapons testing and development have been stopped by everybody—not just India." For years, he points out, "India has been warning that it was unfair and discriminatory for certain nations to maintain nuclear arsenals and to be able to threaten other nations with them."

"If we really want a world free from the horrors of potential nuclear annihilation and free from the economic burdens of an ongoing arms race," Jay Truman says, "the world should choose to get that message and understand it and act on it this time. Because if we don't, we may not get another chance."

May 13, 1998

This Is Your Life, Atomic Flackery!

Born more than fifty years ago as an instant luminary, you're still going strong today. This is your life, Atomic Flackery!

Some call you a has-been. No way. Just the other night, Mr. Flackery, you triumphed again when the PBS program *Frontline* hoisted you on its broad public-TV shoulders. The *New York Times* cheered, and so did the nuclear industry.

But that's nothing new. In the 1950s, you came up with President Eisenhower's oratory about "Atoms for Peace." Ever since, you've been telling Americans not to be scaredy-cats.

During the spring of 1979, you inspired George Will to write a *Newsweek* column denouncing *The China Syndrome*—which dramatized a nuclear reactor accident—as hysterical Hollywood propaganda. "Nuclear plants," he scoffed, "like color-TV sets, give off minute amounts of radiation."

A few days later, however, a lot of people in Pennsylvania stopped laughing at nuclearphobia when the Three Mile Island plant came close to turning much of the state into a nuclear wasteland.

It was a setback, Mr. Flackery. But as a great counter-puncher, you never took unfortunate events lying down. And you're still slugging away.

The *New York Times* has published many dozens of editorials extolling the virtues of nuclear power. So, *Times* television critic Walter Goodman was in sync April 22 [1997] as he praised the *Frontline* nuclear documentary right before it aired on PBS.

Frontline recycled themes from a pro-nuclear hour that NBC News produced in 1987, soon after NBC was bought by General Electric—the nation's second-largest vendor of nuclear-power reactors. These days, CBS News employees are also in no position to scrutinize nuclear matters now that CBS belongs to Westinghouse, another firm heavily invested in atomic power.

TV viewers might have hoped that PBS—"public television"—would be different. But you, Mr. Flackery, didn't miss a beat. Echoing what NBC/GE provided ten years earlier, *Frontline* proclaimed that nuclear power works in France, where people "trust their experts."

The narration was soothing. It contrasted sober "risk analysis" with fearful "risk perception" by "ordinary people." *Frontline* depicted worries about nuclear power as functions of ignorance.

I spoke with the producer in charge of the documentary, Jon Palfreman, the day after it aired. He admitted that he hadn't bothered to interview a single anti-nuclear scientist for the program, which showcased several scientists enthusiastic about nuclear power.

Palfreman told me he'd stuck to "credible, mainstream scientists"—in other words, the ones accepting the rosy assumptions of the nuclear industry.

In the glowing spirit of Mr. Flackery, the *Frontline* narrator Richard Rhodes intoned that "no one was injured or killed in the accident" at Three Mile Island. Later, he widened the assertion: "In America, there have been no deaths or injuries from nuclear accidents in commercial power plants."

But two months before that claim went on the air as supposed fact, the *Washington Post* published a very different news report: "Researchers have linked radiation releases from the Three Mile Island nuclear plant to higher cancer rates in nearby communities."

The findings appeared in the Feb. 24 [1997] edition of the journal of the U.S. National Institute of Environmental Health Science. As the *Post* reported, the study concluded that neighbors who were exposed to radioactive releases "suffered two to ten times as many lung cancer and leukemia cases as those who lived upwind."

When I asked Palfreman about those findings, he said they were not worth mentioning in the *Frontline* documentary.

Also judged irrelevant was the Ukrainian government's estimate of at least 8,000 deaths due to the 1986 Chernobyl nuclear plant disaster. Acknowledgment of that figure would have made it tough for *Frontline* to stick with its script: "The actual death toll from Chernobyl is surprisingly low. Thirty-one firefighters died in the accident. So far, leukemia and adult cancers have not measurably increased."

And so it goes, Mr. Flackery. You're still on the case. And your favorite pro-nuclear hat trick is still in use: *Frontline* showed a piece of paper blocking plutonium's radioactive rays. No need to explain how tiny particles of plutonium, cesium, strontium and many other isotopes do horrendous damage to human bodies if swallowed or inhaled.

This is your life, Atomic Flackery! There's so much more to say about your achievements, but we're out of time.

April 23, 1997

The Partnership for a Candor-Free America

The most famous anti-drug commercial in history—a frying egg and a somber warning, "This is your brain on drugs"—is badly in need of a sequel.

Our new spot opens with a wide-angle shot of a press conference featuring the president of ABC Television. Also in the picture are speakers from the Partnership for a Drug-Free America, plus federal officials in charge of education, health and drug policy.

"This is your nation's leadership on drugs," the announcer intones. "A more sanctimonious and hypocritical bunch you couldn't imagine."

With the help of computer graphics, the dignitaries slowly morph into upscale party-goers. Some are smoking cigarettes, others are sipping cocktails—and all have large checks spilling from their pockets.

"On March 4, 1997, these men and women gathered in Washington to launch yet another 'anti-drug' campaign," the script goes on. "But they continued to tiptoe around the most damaging drugs in our society. As a practical matter, they're flunkies for the multibillion-dollar interests behind cigarettes and alcohol."

You might think that such a public-service ad would be unfair. But consider these facts:

- The U.S. government is providing half the funds for a new $350 million media campaign against drugs. But the advertising drive—which depends on matching donations from media companies—will give short shrift to cigarettes and alcohol.

- This month [March 1997], the ABC television and radio networks are engaged in a "March Against Drugs" programming blitz with little to say about smoking and drinking.

- During the past ten years, the Partnership for a Drug-Free America has produced $2 billion worth of ads. None of them have said an ill word about tobacco or alcohol.

The Partnership depends on free air time and print space. "By far, ABC has contributed more media time and space than any other company," the organization declares. "Our tremendous success over the past decade is a direct reflection of their belief in our cause."

Now, after joining itself at the hip with the Partnership and like-minded federal officials, ABC News is in no position to let the chips fall where they may.

"ABC's March Against Drugs"—which has enlisted such key shows as *Good Morning America* and *World News Tonight*— would more aptly be named "ABC's March Against Journalism."

In a letter to ABC, several drug-policy groups blasted the Partnership: "By excluding any mention of alcohol and tobacco, the implicit message sent to kids and the general public is that legal drugs are not as harmful as illegal drugs." Yet, in the United States, "over 500,000 people die each year from alcohol and tobacco—35 times the number of deaths from all illegal drugs combined."

Mike Males, a sociologist who authored *The Scapegoat Generation*, points out that federal authorities concentrate on bad-mouthing underage use of tobacco and alcohol—thereby enhancing the image of smoking and drinking as "mature" activities.

"Instead of teaming up with political and private drug-war interests to scapegoat young people," Males comments, "ABC and other media would do a far greater public service to investigate at arm's length why the war on drugs is such a monumental failure."

Clearly, finger-wagging techniques don't work. Extensive research—including the U.S. Education Department's recent evaluation of D.A.R.E. programs—proves that "just say no" messages are not effective in reducing drug use among children and adolescents.

Because the Partnership for a Drug-Free America has refused to utter a word against cigarettes or alcohol, news media have found it easier to downplay those major threats to public health. The current anti-drug effort by ABC is a case in point.

When ABC faxed me a dozen pages about this month's special news reports with "anti-drug themes," the only targeted drugs were marijuana, heroin and "sniffing inhalants." The selective coverage will, no doubt, gratify the beer marketers and conglomerates with tobacco holdings that pour huge ad revenues into ABC's coffers.

Talk about addiction! From the network suites of ABC to the Partnership for a Drug-Free America to officialdom in Washington, movers and shakers are hobbled by dependency on this nation's legal drug sellers—the alcohol, tobacco and pharmaceutical firms that are all too happy to focus anti-drug ire elsewhere.

Take a look around. This is your country. This is your country on drugs.

March 5, 1997

News Media Hit Jackpot
With State Lotteries

By now, we're so accustomed to the spectacle of state-run gambling that we rarely give it a second thought.

Lotteries have spread across the country during the last couple of decades. From sea to shining sea, the get-lucky hype is hard to miss.

If people want to gamble, that's their choice. But is it proper for government agencies to constantly exhort the public to buy lottery tickets at supermarkets and liquor stores?

Such questions should be debated. But most news outlets seem too caught up in lottery mania to scrutinize it. Americans get a steady stream of news and feature stories about bulging pots of gold at the end of the lottery rainbow.

Nationwide, a lot of local TV stations report on the state lottery with great enthusiasm. Nightly newscasts announce the winning numbers and the size of the next jackpot. And, of course, we learn about the ecstatic winners who have become instant millionaires.

If you've been reluctant to play the lottery, the state tries hard to promote the idea that you're out of step. Plenty of public-relations expertise goes into creating glamorous images for games like Super Lotto and Powerball.

While few lottery players benefit from their gullibility, many print and broadcast outlets hit the jackpot. Overall, states spend a little more than $1 million per day for lottery advertising.

We're encouraged to go out and buy lottery tickets on the extremely slim chance that lightning will strike. Financially and psychologically, it's quite a rip-off. In the 38 states with lotteries, total sales topped $34 billion in 1996.

The lotteries are touted as a way to fund government services. But, as *Money* magazine has reported, "lotteries are an inefficient way to raise public money"—with two-thirds of sales going to "administrative costs and prizes."

Meanwhile, the media spotlight seldom falls on such matters as compulsive gambling and the regressive nature of collecting revenue from lotteries. Lower-income people are more apt to play the lottery and more likely to suffer as a result.

Many state governments have expanded their gambling operations with flashier offerings and cranked-up promotional campaigns. At the same time, news outlets have remained upbeat about the mirage of lottery salvation.

What the-lottery-changed-my-life stories don't mention is that state-sponsored gambling is no substitute for equitable taxation. Propelling a few lucky players into wealth is a lousy substitute for implementing a fair tax system.

Politicians like to say that lotteries underwrite schools and other commendable government projects—as if generating more tax dollars from large corporations and the wealthy were not an option.

Amid all the media hoopla about miraculous lottery tickets, it would be helpful to hear more about the grim realities of today's tax picture. For instance: During the 1950s, U.S. corporations paid 28 percent of federal revenues. Now, corporations pay just 11 percent.

During the past four decades, the top bracket of marginal tax rates for personal income has plunged from 91.2 percent to the current level of 39.6 percent. Drops in the federal tax rate for the most well-to-do have shifted more of the tax burden onto others.

"The richest taxpayers, who saw their income go up the fastest in the last twenty years, pay fewer taxes than they did two decades ago," points out John Miller, a professor of economics at Wheaton College in Norton, Massachusetts. "In 1996, the top 1 percent paid one-third of their income in federal taxes, well below the two-fifths of their income that went to federal taxes in 1977."

Miller adds that "not all income is taxed and some income is taxed at favorable rates. It is the capital income of the rich—

from capital gains to interest on state and local bonds—that is most often tax-exempt or taxed at more favorable rates."

Rather than take on such issues, it's much easier for politicians and the news media to keep banging the drum for state lotteries. The ads emphasize that we can't win if we don't play. But no matter what, our society keeps losing.

May 6, 1998

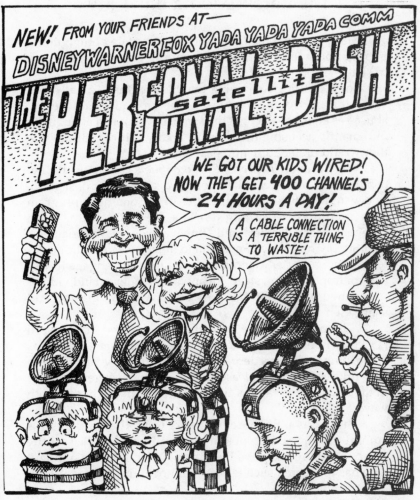

All Hail Jerry Springer,
the Latest Media Bad Guy

Many national media outlets are in a state of high moral outrage about Jerry Springer, the current emperor of daytime trash television.

Some critics are charging that his program—a daily presentation of violence, bleeped-out profanity and verbal abuse—is all too real. Or, at the same time, not real enough. By indignantly accusing the show of fakery, critics indicate that they would prefer authentic sleaziness.

What airs on *The Jerry Springer Show* can be troubling. Sometimes, it may seem like a not-too-distant mirror of anguish, idiocy and confusion. Recent titles of the one-hour program have included "My Daughter Is a Teen Prostitute," "I'm Pregnant by My Brother" and "I'm in a Bizarre Love Triangle."

Supplying plenty of material to titillate viewers, the guests tell salacious stories, denounce each other and engage in violent confrontations on stage. Meanwhile, renowned individuals in the media business can pose on lofty moral ground and shake their heads.

A lot of high-profile head shaking occurred in late April [1998], when ABC's *20/20* and NBC's *Dateline* took turns bemoaning Springer's depravity and greed. Conveniently, both networks chose to broadcast their in-depth Springer coverage in the midst of the ratings sweeps period. Nice to have it both ways.

These days, Springer appears to be the king of TV's amoral profiteers. But, despite his millions, he's just a little prince compared to guys like Barry Diller, the media mogul who has pioneered such televised innovations as home-shopping channels.

Diller is the head of USA Networks Inc., the conglomerate that produces and distributes *The Jerry Springer Show*. While Bad Jerry faces down hostile questions from a wide range of journalists, Good Barry stays out of the line of fire, running his vast media empire.

As the years pass, the Springers are apt to come and go. They're people who function as products. In contrast, the Dillers tend to have much more staying power—and their giant companies keep getting bigger.

Complaints about trash TV never get very far. That's because most commentators—whether they consider themselves to be conservatives, liberals or whatever—are afraid to challenge the "principle" of the so-called free market.

Of course, the free market is a myth. Media titans like Diller or Rupert Murdoch—and corporate outfits such as Time Warner, Disney and Viacom—have a lock on huge portions of the mass media.

Steadily larger in size and fewer in number, the dominant biggies are fixated on doing whatever it takes to boost profits. They're not about to sacrifice any appreciable part of profit margins on behalf of the public interest.

Do media tycoons like Diller and blow-dried hirelings like Springer just give the public what it wants? "That is the biggest fallacy in our business," TV journalist Linda Ellerbee retorted a decade ago. "That's the argument that people on our side use to put dreck on the air."

People sitting in front of TV sets do not choose from what isn't available. They choose from what is.

"The American public didn't ask for trash television," Ellerbee pointed out. "They'll watch it the same way we go out and watch a fire. It's not all they want."

Now, as arguments fly about *The Jerry Springer Show*, insights are diluted by abundant quantities of hogwash.

Yes, some of the show's critics are "elitist." They're put off by low-income, unschooled people who don't have the social graces usually regarded as minimal for the airwaves.

But Springer's defenders are absurd when they wrap his program in a populist flag. Such TV shows are caricatures.

The people on stage are carefully selected to fit a script that stereotypes rather than illuminates. Relatively few Americans are "qualified" to make it onto Jerry Springer's stage. The producers work awfully hard to find them.

Meanwhile, Springer and his bosses like to act as though they pay respect to working-class Americans by putting these parodies on the nation's TV screens. But they're not doing anyone a favor—except Barry Diller and his rich pals.

April 29, 1998

Part XV
Picking and Choosing
the World's Human Rights

U.S. Media Miscast as
Human-Rights Watchdogs

During Hong Kong's first days under the Chinese flag, many American journalists speculated on the future of human rights in the former British colony.

As the royal yacht Britannia sped away from Hong Kong, network anchors worried aloud. A front-page *New York Times* headline asked: "Will Beijing Honor Vows?" And so on.

The news coverage might leave the impression that U.S. media outlets are vigilant watchdogs for human rights in other countries. That's a pleasant image—but it has little to do with reality.

For instance, the media establishment in the United States has barely stifled a yawn at the Western Hemisphere's worst ongoing human-rights disaster. In Colombia, many lives are shadowed by carnage:

- Journalism is a hazardous profession for Colombians. Last spring [1997], attackers took the lives of newspaper editor Gerardo Bedoya and photographer Freddy Ahumada. The U.S.-based Committee to Protect Journalists cites "evidence of renewed violence."

  The committee says that Colombia's journalists face "death threats, physical attack, bombings and kidnapping at the hands of a broad range of players—drug barons, the military, paramilitary groups and guerrilla terrorists—all intent on silencing them."

- While receiving $169 million in annual military aid from Washington, the Bogota government maintains direct ties with paramilitary death squads in the Colombian countryside. Abductions, torture and grisly mutilations are common. Punishment is rare.

A Human Rights Watch report—released in autumn 1996 but virtually ignored by the U.S. press—showed that the Clinton administration is equipping "killer networks" operated by Colombian military and paramilitary units.

- The media myth is that drug traffickers are to blame for most of Colombia's murder and mayhem. Guerrilla insurgents, who are guilty of atrocities, also get a lot of bad press.

  But independent monitors, such as the Colombian Commission of Jurists, have documented that the government's army, police and allied armed groups commit about two-thirds of Colombia's political murders—which occur at an average rate of eleven per day. Among those killed in recent years: more than 3,000 elected members of the alternative Union Patriotica party.

- "The most atrocious violence that we are experiencing comes from the state and its secret affiliates, which are the paramilitary groups," says Father Javier Giraldo. He's a Jesuit priest who heads the Inter-Congregational Commission for Justice and Peace, a panel formed by fifty-five Catholic religious orders in Colombia.

  Father Giraldo points out that "the United States continues sending military aid to our government without conditioning it on respect for basic human rights."

Irked at Colombian President Ernesto Samper's drug policies, Washington halted some assistance to his government. But the cutoff didn't interrupt the flow of U.S. aid to Colombia's military and police.

In theory, the Yankee dollars are earmarked for anti-drug efforts—but in practice, they fund militarized repression aimed largely at popular organizations, labor unions and the poor. For good measure, the Pentagon and U.S. intelligence agencies keep hundreds of advisers in Colombia.

Such aid is reassuring to foreigners with a huge economic stake in Colombia. These days, the country's biggest legal export isn't coffee—it's oil. Companies like Texaco, Chevron and Occidental Petroleum are heavily invested.

The *Wall Street Journal* noted in 1996 that U.S. firms "are responsible for more than half of all foreign direct investment in the country." As far as they're concerned, Colombia's status quo is worthy of protection.

In contrast to Hong Kong's uncertainties, some nightmarish realities arrived long ago in Colombia—where violence takes about 35,000 lives yearly in a country of 37 million people.

The shortage of U.S. media attention to those realities is especially tragic because the Colombian military is hypersensitive to negative publicity in the United States.

A few months ago, a high-ranking Colombian officer, General Rito del Rio, angrily denounced a World Wide Web site operated by the Colombia Support Network based in Madison, Wisconsin. The factual human-rights information on the Web—at www.igc.org/csn—has infuriated commanders of the Colombian armed forces.

But the top brass of Colombia's murderous military don't have much to complain about when it comes to U.S. media coverage of human rights.

July 2, 1997

Media and Memory:
The Arrest of a Dictator

The arrest of General Augusto Pinochet in mid-October [1998] presented a challenge to American news media. For a quarter of a century—after a bloody coup brought Pinochet to power in Chile—he didn't get much bad press in the United States. As time went on, it seemed that human memory had been buried alive. But Pinochet's arrest suddenly exhumed the legacies of his seventeen-year dictatorship.

National Public Radio news analyst Daniel Schorr pointed out on Oct. 19 that Pinochet seized control of Chile "after the CIA had organized a campaign to destabilize the democratically elected but left-leaning Salvador Allende." And Schorr identified another key orchestrator of the 1973 coup—Henry Kissinger, who coordinated foreign policy for President Nixon.

But overall, American journalists have dodged the crucial roles of the CIA and Kissinger (still a media darling). Five days after Pinochet was arrested in London, a search of the Nexis database found that out of 806 major English-language news stories on the subject, only thirty-four had mentioned the CIA. Kissinger fared even better: Just six stories mentioned him, and only two of those were in U.S. media.

Meanwhile, some coverage grotesquely understated the horrors of the Pinochet regime. The first sentence of the front-page *New York Times* report on Pinochet's arrest declared that he "came to symbolize the excesses of military rule in Latin America." Mass murder and widespread torture are merely "excesses"?

A range of daily papers weighed in with cogent editorials. "Justice may yet have its day," said the *Chicago Tribune*, which hailed the arrest. The *Los Angeles Times* was more skeptical of legal precedents but nevertheless concluded: "Finally we hear the wheels of justice turning." The *New York Times* commented that "his detention and possible prosecution are warranted under international law."

But top editors at two influential newspapers clearly hated to see Pinochet in custody. The *Wall Street Journal* went ballistic as it decried the injustice being done to Chile's "former strongman." The *Washington Post* also sounded quite distressed.

"He did remove a democratically elected government and see to the killing of thousands and the detention of tens of thousands in 1973–1990," the *Post* noted, but "he also saw to the rescue of his country." The editorial added: "It is not only Chile's military right but others grateful for his positive role who are troubled now by his arrest in the British hospital he had sought out for back surgery. He is 82."

But thousands of Chileans never had a chance to come anywhere near age 82—thanks to General Pinochet and his "positive role."

In stark contrast to the euphemisms on this side of the Atlantic, the *Guardian* newspaper supplied British readers with succinct history: "Salvador Allende, the first democratically elected Marxist in Latin America when he was elected president in November 1970, presented an ideological and economic affront to the Nixon regime... Nixon tried to prevent Allende's victory by ordering the CIA to 'make the economy scream.' Later, Kissinger told the CIA that 'it is firm and continuing policy that Allende should be overthrown by a coup.' Three years later he had his way and Allende was dead."

Allende led a "Popular Unity" government that was dedicated to social uplift. It brought nutrition, health care, education and employment to millions of impoverished people in Chile. It broke new ground by ensuring that poor children had milk to drink. And it deepened democratic processes for much of Chilean society.

Almost without exception, news accounts give short shrift to the three years of enlivening changes that abruptly ended with the coup on Sept. 11, 1973. The suppression of memory has included the blanking out of vibrant and humanizing values nurtured during the Popular Unity era.

"The most premeditated manifestation of forgetting is depoliticization," Chilean sociology professor Tomas Moulian wrote recently. "It is also the most pernicious, as it saps the strength of social solidarity."

By now, Moulian observed, Chile has come to resemble "societies that do not seek to transform themselves and have become trapped by the dullness of repetition. They no longer think in terms of emancipation because they believe that the system itself produces a degree of equality that no other social system can attain."

In Chile, and in the United States, the memory of other possibilities is also gasping for breath.

October 21, 1998

Poor Journalism South of the Border

Filled with speeches and photo-ops, President Clinton's visit to Mexico [in May 1997] produced a lot of good press back home. Most journalists sang the official tunes about immigration, drugs and corruption. The few off-key notes didn't last long, as when ABC's Peter Jennings reported: "This is where the U.S. gets cheap labor and makes enormous manufacturing profits."

Perhaps you saw TV footage of Mexican people living in dire poverty. But it's unlikely that you heard much about *why* so many are so poor. If the network's roving correspondents knew why, they avoided spilling the beans.

But not all the U.S. reporters arrived and left with Clinton. One of the few who actually lives in Mexico is John Ross, a freelance journalist who has been covering Latin America for sixteen years. He's committed to probing beyond the conventional media wisdom.

When I reached him in Mexico City during Clinton's trip, Ross began by pointing out that "Mexico is a country where 158,000 babies annually do not survive their fifth year due to nutritionally related disease. Two million more infants are seriously harmed by underfeeding."

The crisis, he stressed, is growing more severe. "As many as 40 percent of all Mexicans suffer from some degree of undernutrition. And a report by Banamex, the nation's top private bank, indicates that half of Mexico's 92 million citizens are eating less than the minimum daily requirement of 1,300 calories as a result of the deepest recession since 1932."

Imagine the human realities behind the dry statistics: "Mexico's basic grain consumption dropped by 29 percent in 1995," Ross says, "and meat and milk consumption has slipped by an alarming 60 percent and 40 percent respectively during the last three years. The price of tortillas, the staple of poor people's diets, has doubled in the past 18 months."

President Clinton's upbeat visit to Mexico is now history. And so is the superficial sheen put on that event by U.S. mass media.

Ross—who wrote the award-winning 1995 book *Rebellion From the Roots: Indian Uprising in Chiapas*—refuses to polish the sheen. Instead, he tells about places like the town of San Agustin Loxicha in southern Mexico, "where poverty is so extreme that babies die in the priests' arms during baptism."

The town is in a region that supplies coffee beans to cafés in my neighborhood and yours.

Those who challenge the conditions in Loxicha face an iron fist, Ross explains: "Fifty of Loxicha's most upstanding citizens, including most of the town government and seven of its teachers, are penned up just outside the Oaxaca state capital, at the riot-scarred Santa Maria Ixcotel penitentiary, behind thick black steel doors in two cramped cells." The pending charge is armed rebellion.

Ross adds that "the prisoners tell of classic torture by authorities—their heads were wrapped in rags and dirty water poured into their mouths; electric wires were attached to their genitals; they were threatened with being hurled from helicopters into the ocean."

Far from media spotlights, the Mexican military—wielding U.S. equipment—is on the march to bolster the status quo, Ross reports. In Oaxaca, the routine includes "forced interrogations, widespread use of torture, secret prisons and kidnappings of prominent citizens, according to a report filed in February [1997] by the Mexican League for the Defense of Human Rights, the state's most active independent human rights group."

Today, at least 60,000 troops are deployed across broad terrain to crush resistance. In Ross's words: "From the Huasteca mountains, an impoverished, coffee-growing range that stretches through five states in eastern Mexico, all the way to the Lacandon jungle on the Guatemalan border, the Mexican army moves through indigenous zones, setting up road blocks, conducting house-to-house searches, arbitrarily beating and incarcerating Indians."

Meanwhile, Ross says, 27 million Mexican people still labor—against worsening odds—to scratch the soil for a living. They do so "despite a decade of decapitalizing the agrarian sector to conform with International Monetary Fund strictures, huge imports of cheap NAFTA grain that is driving small farmers off the land in droves, and forced 'association' with transnational agribusiness that gobbles whole farming communities."

Do you think such information belongs on the evening news?

May 7, 1997

Netanyahu Benefits From Chronic Media Bias

When Israel's prime minister arrived in Washington [on Feb. 12, 1997], he stepped into friendly media territory.

Benjamin Netanyahu basked in accolades for finally agreeing to an Israeli pullback from the West Bank city of Hebron. Even former detractors offered praise. "We have been wrong about him," concluded *Washington Post* columnist Richard Cohen, who applauded "a commitment from Netanyahu to the peace process."

And so it goes. With feeble critics easily assuaged in the U.S. press corps, Netanyahu can proceed with a "peace process" that has little to do with justice.

Although news coverage may get a bit cool when Netanyahu displeases American policy-makers, there's scant danger that Israel will fall from media grace in the United States. Any problems with public relations are apt to be brief.

Netanyahu, who graduated from the Massachusetts Institute of Technology, knows the lay of the media land in this country. For several years during the 1980s, he served as the Israeli ambassador to the United Nations. His TV skills were honed on programs like ABC's *Nightline*.

These days, many news stories are casting Netanyahu as a potential hero of the "peace process." The grim details of his partnership with the head of the Palestinian Authority, Yasser Arafat, don't seem to matter much. In effect, the two leaders share the task of suppressing Palestinians who oppose their pact.

Five years ago, in east Jerusalem, I visited editors of a Palestinian newspaper going through the daily ordeal of submitting page proofs to Israeli censors. Lately, the censorship chores have fallen to Arafat's henchmen.

Palestinians are also suffering more extreme measures. Investigators for Human Rights Watch report "recurrent"

Israeli practices "such as torture, arbitrary and prolonged detention without charge or trial, and wholesale restrictions on movement of people amounting to collective punishment." Meanwhile, Arafat's police are torturing and sometimes murdering prisoners.

But U.S. media attention to these human-rights abuses is minimal and fleeting. American news outlets—long accustomed to giving the Israeli government the benefit of the doubt—now tacitly assume that Arafat is engaged in worthy endeavors when he serves the interests of Israel and the U.S. government.

We're so familiar with pro-Israel media bias that it may seem natural. But far more evenhanded coverage is possible, as regular monitoring of Britain's BBC Radio confirms. The contrast with our National Public Radio is striking.

America's routine news accounts don't shed light on the extensive control that Israel retains over the land it has occupied since the 1967 war. In the West Bank, the isolated Palestinian enclaves resemble South Africa's apartheid-era "bantustans."

Even further Israeli withdrawals won't change the fact that Israel's soldiers can restrict travel and commerce between the scattered Palestinian towns. At the same time, essential resources like water go primarily to Israeli settlements, which continue to expand.

Like any other nation, Israel should be held to high standards of human rights. And Americans have a special reason for concern: The U.S. government is sending more than $3 billion of annual aid to Israel.

One of the trusty arguments used by Israel's boosters is that it's anti-Semitic to criticize the Jewish state. That's nonsense.

Anti-Jewish bigotry can be found among Israel's foes— and backers. For instance, as Oval Office tapes attest, Richard Nixon was prone to anti-Semitism even while he strongly supported Israel and expressed admiration for its military prowess.

In the United States, mainline Jewish organizations claim to speak for virtually all Jews. In a recent full-page *New York Times* ad, the United Jewish Appeal proclaimed: "The seeds of Jewish life and Jewish communities everywhere begin in Israel."

But Israel's fervent enthusiasts drown out the voices of the sizable minority of American Jews who are appalled by the repressive character of modern Israel. As for Arab Americans, their outlooks have little media standing here.

So, Benjamin Netanyahu doesn't have to worry about journalism in the United States. Despite occasional sniping, he can count on America's big media guns to back up Israel, right or wrong.

February 12, 1997

Media Infatuated
With Madeleine Albright

Madeleine Albright may have charmed Jesse Helms on her way to Senate confirmation as secretary of state, but she was merely flirting with a powerful lawmaker. Her real political love affair is with the national press corps.

As she glided to the top job at the State Department, both *Time* and *Newsweek* described Albright as "media-savvy." She now elicits reverence from many journalists transfixed with her new superstardom as the highest-ranking woman ever in the U.S. government.

These days, old friends on the media mound are pleased to lob slow-pitch questions at Albright—and then lavish praise on her ability to hit them out of the park. It's not too tough to awe journalists who are eager to be impressed.

Before she began her four-year stint as U.N. ambassador in 1993, Albright was a regular analyst for the *MacNeil/Lehrer NewsHour* on PBS. When Bill Clinton named her to be secretary of state, the *NewsHour* reported with pride: "Her ease in explaining American foreign policy, which President Clinton mentioned in his remarks today, was honed partly on the *NewsHour*."

Albright provides tasty sound bites for reporters and news consumers who relish glib lines-of-the-day. Taunting Saddam Hussein and Fidel Castro has become one of her specialties. But she never seems to muster any outrage at repressive regimes that the White House looks upon with favor—whether China, Turkey or Saudi Arabia.

Perhaps because she's adept at lacquering her hard-edged rhetoric with a humanitarian gloss, many liberal commentators express fondness for Albright. In a typical testimonial, columnist Christopher Matthews called her latest promotion "a tonic to the country's mood."

A lot of pundits have depicted Albright's ascension as a breakthrough for feminism. In the same spirit, Sen. Dianne Feinstein of California asserted that Albright's rise to secretary of state "will open up new doors for women—not just in this country but around the world."

Top officials of the National Organization for Women joined with leaders of other influential feminist groups, in the fall of 1996, to pressure the White House on behalf of Albright—and then claimed credit as soon as she got the president's nod. This is the kind of narrow, shortsighted "feminism" that confuses symbols with substance.

Across the globe, poverty is especially devastating for women. Meanwhile—now more than ever—Albright is implementing the edicts of an administration that has put harsh economic agendas at the center of its foreign policy. In practice, that has meant pushing and cajoling Third World governments to cut public-sector subsidies for food, health care, housing and education.

These "reform" measures are being promoted by the State Department as well as global agencies like the World Bank and the International Monetary Fund. Their prescriptions are popular with investors. But poor women and families the world over are bearing the brunt of policies that slash at already-threadbare safety nets.

"We are not a charity or a fire department," Albright said recently. "We will defend firmly our own vital interests." Left unexamined by news coverage are crucial questions: Whose "vital interests" is she talking about? Who's being protected—Wall Street or most Americans?

Neither mainstream journalists nor Albright's feminist boosters seem interested in exploring who profits and who suffers as this nation's diplomatic bandwagon rolls forward. When it comes to issues that many liberals and women's groups profess to be passionate about, Albright is well situated to get a free ride.

More curious observers might wonder why key members of former President Reagan's foreign-policy team—such as U.N.

Ambassador Jeane Kirkpatrick and Secretary of State George Shultz—have gone out of their way to praise Albright as a fine choice to run the State Department.

Albright is quite good at playing to the media—and she is acutely aware of their importance. During her tenure as U.N. ambassador, she referred to CNN as "the 16th member of the Security Council." The day after being sworn in as secretary of state, she appeared as a guest on CNN's *Larry King Live*.

Madeleine Albright may be media-savvy. But, under the circumstances, that's hardly cause for celebration.

January 29, 1997

When "Economic Freedom"
Bars Chewing Gum

America's top business newspaper puts out a fascinating document called the *Index of Economic Freedom*. It's a thick book that illuminates the priorities of *Wall Street Journal* editors, who team up with the influential Heritage Foundation to rank the countries of the world.

So, for 1997, which sovereign nation scored highest in economic liberty?

The answer: Singapore.

In Singapore, the indexers of "economic freedom" have seen the future, and it works: "an efficient, strike-free labor force...no minimum wage...no antitrust regulations."

But some significant facts go unmentioned. For instance, chewing gum has been illegal in Singapore since 1992. The government recently reaffirmed the ban and warned citizens that ordering gum from foreign mail catalogs could bring a year in jail and a fine of $6,173.

The crackdown came after authorities blamed wads of gum for jamming subway doors. Evidently, the visionary leaders of Singapore have realized that people can't have economic freedom and chew gum at the same time.

Nor do financial liberties on the Asian island extend to anyone who might want to buy or sell—or read—a copy of *Watchtower* magazine. The Jehovah's Witness religious group and its literature have been banned in Singapore for a quarter of a century.

Throughout 1996, at least forty Jehovah's Witnesses were behind bars in Singapore for refusing military service on religious grounds. Amnesty International calls them "prisoners of conscience." Dozens of other Jehovah's Witnesses spent weeks in jail for "peacefully exercising their right to freedom of expression."

The unfettered commerce that dazzled the "economic freedom" indexers does not include the exchange of ideas or information. As the Associated Press reported, Singapore "has some of the world's strictest media controls."

And Singapore's methods of punishment remain harsh. Brutal caning is mandatory for vandalism and thirty other crimes. Death by hanging awaits those caught with 500 grams of marijuana. As you might guess, dictator Lee Kuan Yew has scorned "decadent" notions of civil liberties.

Ranked just behind Singapore—and also classified as "free" in the *Index of Economic Freedom*—is Bahrain. The small Persian Gulf country wins profuse accolades: "a free-market economic system...no taxes on income or corporate profits...no capital gains tax...few barriers to foreign investment...a vibrant and competitive banking market with few government restrictions."

Overall, in Bahrain, "businesses are free to operate as they see fit." To investors, that's high praise indeed. But you wouldn't know from the report that Bahrain is a traditional monarchy. Long ruled by the al-Khalifa family, it's a nation that gives plutocracy a bad name.

A royal decree abolished Bahrain's parliament twenty-two years ago, and since then the government has suppressed dissent. During the mid-1990s, several thousand people were arrested for pro-democracy street protests. Amnesty International notes that Bahrain's recent political detainees have included "children as young as 10."

In Bahrain, the past year has brought "large-scale and indiscriminate arrests," says Human Rights Watch. "Serious, extensive and recurrent human-rights abuses continued in the form of arbitrary detention, abusive treatment of prisoners and denial of due-process rights." Torture has been common. But "there were no known instances of officials being held accountable."

Clearly, political tyranny can be quite compatible with the kind of economic order favored by folks at the *Wall Street Journal* and the Heritage Foundation. The touting of countries like

Singapore and Bahrain is proof that one-dimensional fixations are foolish—and dangerous.

Despite persistent efforts by some media outlets and think tanks, it's not possible to credibly separate the flow of money from the exercise of power. Every day, much of the real world is buffeted by a political version of the golden rule: Those who have the gold make the rules.

All too often, terms like "economic freedom" get defined in ways that just so happen to favor the interests of the wealthy few. In the process, such definitions set aside democratic values.

Inadvertently, the *Index of Economic Freedom* renders a valuable public service. It shows that narrow concepts of "economic freedom" can be catastrophic for genuine human freedom.

January 22, 1997

Part XVI
Boosting Corporate-Backed
Think Tanks

Ménage à Trois:
Cato, Murdoch, Malone

In the autumn of 1997, when News Corporation owner Rupert Murdoch joined the board of directors at the Cato Institute, the announcement went unreported in major media. Perhaps it seemed routine for one of the world's most powerful media moguls to take a leadership post at one of the most influential think tanks in Washington.

At future meetings, Murdoch can count on rubbing elbows with a fellow media titan, John C. Malone—president and CEO of Tele-Communications Inc. (TCI), the largest cable operator in the United States—who has been on the Cato board since 1995. The two men are well acquainted. Their companies have long been intertwined in media deals involving satellite television, cable-TV systems, program distribution and other big telecommunications ventures. Now the heads of both firms are formally helping to run a think tank which boasts that it has "actively promoted the deregulation of the television and telephone industries."

In recent years, the Cato Institute has neared the top tier of think tanks in the United States—on Capitol Hill and in the nation's news media. In the 1996 book *No Mercy: How Conservative Think Tanks and Foundations Changed America's Social Agenda*, Jean Stefancic and Richard Delgado write that the Cato Institute "has played a key role in forming the ideas and policies of the new Republican majority in Congress." These days, "congressional committee chairmen increasingly look to Cato scholars for testimony."

When FAIR did a search of major newspapers and broadcast outlets in the Nexis computer data base, the media watch group found that Cato was one of four think tanks with more than 1,000 citations in 1995 and again in 1996 [as well as 1997]. The Brookings Institution and the Heritage Foundation were in a virtual tie for first place; Cato followed closely behind third-place American Enterprise Institute.

By the time the Cato Institute celebrated its 20th anniversary at a Washington Hilton bash with 2,000 guests, the *Washington Post* (May 2, 1997) was declaring that "Cato is now the hot policy shop." The *Post* quoted one of the enthusiastic guests, ABC News correspondent John Stossel: "I have no official political affiliation, but I sure seem to be agreeing with them on a lot of things." (A year earlier, Stossel had been the keynote speaker at a Cato "City Seminar" in New York.) For corporations eager to stoke the pro-privatization and anti-regulation fervor of the Cato Institute, it's clearly a good investment.

Broadcasters like Murdoch benefit greatly from federal giveaways. Holding frequency licenses worth fortunes, they're now receiving free slices of a digital spectrum valued at up to $70 billion. Likewise, cable-TV conglomerates—with Malone's TCI in the lead—continue to expand under the protection of federal regulations that place severe limits on the power of municipalities to charge franchise fees for use of public rights-of-way. While lauding the "free market," Murdoch and Malone rely on the federal government's aid in their quest for media monopolization. The contradiction doesn't seem to bother the Cato Institute at all.

While it has criticized "corporate welfare," Cato is much more serious about eliminating government programs for the poor. The annual report for 1996 trumpets a statement by Cato's director of Health and Welfare Studies, Michael Tanner, that "welfare has failed and cannot be reformed. It is time to end it. In its place, the civil society would rely on a reinvigorated network of private charity."

One of Cato's luminaries is José Piñera, co-chair of its Project on Social Security Privatization. According to Cato's latest annual report, "the project's work was cited by nearly every major newspaper in the United States, including the *Washington Post*, the *New York Times*, the *Los Angeles Times*, and the *Wall Street Journal*." The report says that Piñera, a former minister of labor and welfare in Chile, "oversaw the privatization of Chile's

pension system in the early 1980s"—but does not mention that at the time the Chilean government was under the dictatorship of General Augusto Pinochet. Evidently, Cato's concern about intrusive government does not extend to torture and murder.

In terms of commitment to human rights, Cato has found a kindred spirit in Rupert Murdoch, who is fond of floating lofty rhetoric about his Star TV satellite network. "Satellite broadcasting makes it possible for information-hungry residents of many closed societies to bypass state-controlled television," said Murdoch, who touts new media technology as a "threat to totalitarian regimes everywhere." But Murdoch quickly kowtowed to China's totalitarian regime when Beijing objected to Star TV transmissions of BBC News reports about Chinese human rights abuses. In 1994, Murdoch's network dropped the BBC from its broadcasts to Asia. "The BBC was driving them nuts," Murdoch said. "It's not worth it."

Murdoch sits on the board of directors of Philip Morris, the tobacco giant recently inducted into INFACT's Hall of Shame "for exerting undue influence over public policy-making" with the help of 240 registered federal and state lobbyists—often spending upwards of $2 million per month to lobby federal officials. Murdoch publications such as *TV Guide* reap enormous profits from cigarette ads. And Murdoch's Fox Broadcasting is cozy with Philip Morris subsidiary Miller Brewing Company, which recently boosted its advertising account with Fox to about $75 million per year for sports and prime-time programs.

But Murdoch is just one of many Cato links to Big Tobacco. Although news reporting and media commentaries often include the Cato Institute's assessments of tobacco-related issues, Cato's direct ties to tobacco rarely get mentioned. For years, the list of Cato's large contributors has included Philip Morris Companies and R.J. Reynolds Company.

As it happens, Cato is a fierce tiger when it comes to advocating for oppressed tobacco firms. In June 1997, a Cato "Policy Analysis" by senior fellow Robert A. Levy denounced state lawsuits against tobacco companies to recover Medicaid costs for treating people with smoking-related diseases. He claimed that anti-tobacco politicians were "willing to deny due process to a single industry selected for its deep pockets and public image rather than its legal culpability."

Testifying before the Senate Judiciary Committee a month later, Levy sounded a similar theme—calling a proposed tobacco settlement "a shameful document, extorted by public officials who have perverted the rule of law to tap the deep pockets of a feckless and friendless industry." For good measure, Levy excoriated newly proposed restrictions on tobacco advertising as "draconian." And he went ballistic over the idea that tobacco firms should provide funds for the health care of children without insurance: "To hold a single industry financially liable is no more than a bald transfer of wealth from a disfavored to a favored group."

Such pronouncements from the lips of tobacco company lawyers are likely to be taken with outsized grains of salt by the public. But Levy, whose title is "senior fellow in constitutional studies at the Cato Institute," has consistently received respectful media coverage—without reference to the links between the tobacco industry he defends and the think tank that employs him.

So, in a news article that appeared on July 10, 1997—a week before Levy testified on Capitol Hill—the *Chicago Tribune* devoted several paragraphs to Levy's views, quoting his claims that federal efforts to regulate tobacco have been counterproductive. The article identified the Cato Institute only as "a libertarian think tank in the capital"—though it could have just as accurately been described as an advocacy group paid by the tobacco industry.

The next month, on Aug. 31, when the *San Diego Union-Tribune* published an 1,100-word op-ed article by Levy under the headline "Rule of Law Is a Loser in Tobacco War," the bio blurb mentioned Levy's post at Cato—but not Cato's relationship with tobacco companies. In that piece, Levy ("a senior fellow in constitutional studies at the Cato Institute") lambasted "an $11 billion settlement of Florida's war against the tobacco industry." He called the settlement "shameful" because "it strips a currently unfashionable industry of basic protections the rest of us take for granted." Ten days later, in *USA Today*, Levy surfaced again as a concerned legal scholar writing an opinion piece that decried the persecution of tobacco firms and blasted "our pervasive regulatory state."

Major media outlets have routinely turned a blind eye to the corporate financial backing for Cato and other large think tanks in Washington. Few reporters or pundits focus on the conflicts of interests involved.

In 1996, a report by Public Citizen illuminated the industry money behind the major think tanks campaigning to strip regulatory authority from the Food and Drug Administration. "Seven think tanks—the American Enterprise Institute, the Cato Institute, the Competitive Enterprise Institute, the Heritage Foundation, the Hudson Institute, the Progress and Freedom Foundation and the Washington Legal Foundation—received at least $3.5 million between 1992 and 1995 from drug, medical device, biotechnology and tobacco manufacturers and their corporate foundations." But mainstream journalists paid scant attention to who was paying the piper. "Some of the country's most renowned think tanks, frequently cited by the American media, are carrying water for the drug, medical device, biotechnology and tobacco industries."

Not all daily papers have dodged those realities. Under the headline "FDA's Detractors Get Funny Funding," the *Tennessean* commented on July 29, 1996: "The think tanks named in the report, including the Cato Institute, the Heritage Foundation and the American Enterprise Institute, have produced a steady stream of anti-FDA sentiment, including op-ed pieces and reports over the last several years." The newspaper noted "a tremendous difference between an independent think tank, which does legitimate research, and a quasi-academic mouthpiece financed by a regulated industry."

Clearly, the Cato Institute falls in the latter category. The Institute's yearly funding has climbed above $8 million, more than twice what it was in 1992. The organization's most recent annual report exults: "We've moved into a beautiful new $13.7 million headquarters at 1000 Massachusetts Avenue and have only $1 million in debt remaining on it as we enter 1997." Dozens of huge corporations, eager to roll back government regulatory powers, are among Cato's largest donors.

In their book *No Mercy*, University of Colorado Law School scholars Stefancic and Delgado describe a shift in Cato's patron base over the years. Cato's main philanthropic backing has come from the right-wing Koch, Lambe and Sarah Scaife foundations. But today, Cato "receives most of its financial support from entrepreneurs, securities and commodities traders, and corporations such as oil and gas companies, Federal Express, and Philip Morris that abhor government regulation."

Financial firms now kicking in big checks to Cato include American Express, Chase Manhattan Bank, Chemical Bank, Citicorp/Citibank, Commonwealth Fund and Prudential Securities. Energy conglomerates: Chevron Companies, Exxon Company, Shell Oil Company and Tennaco Gas, as well as the American Petroleum Institute, Amoco Foundation and Atlantic Richfield Foundation. Cato's pharmaceutical donors include Eli Lilly & Company, Merck & Company and Pfizer, Inc.

While serving on Cato's board and making personal donations, TCI's John Malone is among many media heavies behind Cato. Big donors include Bell Atlantic Network Services, BellSouth Corporation, Digital Equipment Corporation, GTE Corporation, Microsoft Corporation, Netscape Communications Corporation, NYNEX Corporation, Sun Microsystems and Viacom International. It's understandable that Cato's news releases—while constantly urging privatization of the Internet and other communications systems—do not mention where Cato money is coming from. But it's inexcusable that media coverage seldom includes such information.

Announcing that Murdoch had joined its board, a Cato news release praised him as "a strong advocate of the free market" and quoted his stirring words—"I start from a simple principle: in every area of economic activity in which competition is attainable, it is much to be preferred to monopoly." Cato cited a speech that Murdoch had made eight years earlier, proclaiming that "across the world there is a realization that only market economies can deliver both political freedom and economic well-being."

Murdoch is a global media giant whose U.S. possessions include the Fox television network, *TV Guide*, the tabloid *New York Post*, HarperCollins book publishers and the Twentieth Century Fox movie studios. Along the way, lax federal regulation has swelled the profits of Murdoch's News Corporation, now a $28 billion conglomerate. As a spring 1997 *New York Times* article noted, his ten-year-old Fox TV network "could never have succeeded if it had not received generous treatment at the Federal Communications Commission."

Naturally, turning such big governmental wheels requires lots of political grease. In 1996, Murdoch donated $1 million to the California Republican Party, while News Corporation gave another $654,700 in "soft money" to the national GOP. In Murdoch's native Australia, News Corporation dominates the mass media. In Britain, Murdoch controls more than a third of daily newspaper circulation along with much of cable and satellite television. While using his media outlets to push for the slashing of government social services, Murdoch was a pioneer of union-busting in the newspaper industry.

Murdoch is likely to have a long and harmonious presence on the Cato Institute's board of directors.

January 1998

Launching Pad for Authors:
The Manhattan Institute

When Abigail Thernstrom became a national media star as a scholarly foe of affirmative action, it was yet another triumph for the Manhattan Institute. Once again, its "Book Fellowship Program" had launched an author into the media stratosphere.

A senior fellow at the Manhattan Institute, Thernstrom credits the think tank for "unwavering commitment" to her 1997 book *America in Black and White*, co-written with husband Stephan Thernstrom. In addition, the authors thank five right-wing funders: "The John M. Olin Foundation, the Lynde and Harry Bradley Foundation, the Smith Richardson Foundation, the Earhart Foundation and the Carthage Foundation have also generously funded our research."

The Manhattan Institute was founded in 1978 by William Casey, who later became President Reagan's CIA director. Since then, the Institute's track record with authors has been notable. Funneling money from very conservative foundations, the Institute has sponsored books by many writers opposed to safety-net social programs and affirmative action. During the 1980s, the Institute's authors included George Gilder (*Wealth and Poverty*), Linda Chavez (*Out of the Barrio*) and Charles Murray (*Losing Ground*).

Of course, the funders behind the Thernstroms' book have not confined themselves to routing money to authors via the Manhattan Institute. For instance, the Bradley and Smith Richardson foundations gave sizeable grants to *New York Times* reporter Richard Bernstein for his 1994 book denouncing multiculturalism, *Dictatorship of Virtue*. (Bernstein is now a book reviewer at the *Times*.) But through the years, the Manhattan Institute has proved to be a key conduit for turning book projects into media sensations.

Charles Murray's book *Losing Ground*—a denunciation of social programs for the poor—catapulted him to media stardom in 1984. More than a dozen years later, in October 1997, the *Philadelphia Inquirer* recalled that *Losing Ground* "provided much of the intellectual groundwork for welfare reform." As Murray wrote in the book's preface, the decision by Manhattan Institute officials to subsidize the book project was crucial: "Without them, the book would not have been written."

Murray became a national figure only after joining the Manhattan Institute as a Bradley Fellow. In 1982, the think tank "offered the then-unknown Murray a position as a senior research fellow and the Institute's full financial backing to complete *Losing Ground*," recount Jean Stefancic and Richard Delgado of the University of Colorado Law School. "The Institute raised $125,000 to promote Murray's book and pay him a $35,000 stipend, most coming from Scaife [Foundation], which gave $75,000, and Olin, $25,000. Upon publication, it sent 700 free copies to academics, journalists, and public officials worldwide, sponsored seminars on the book, and funded a nationwide speaking tour for Murray that was made possible by a $15,000 grant from the Liberty Fund."

The largesse from right-wing funders yielded big results. By early 1985, Murray's book had become a widely touted brief against spending tax dollars on low-income people. "This year's budget-cutters' bible seems to be *Losing Ground*," said a *New York Times* editorial in February 1985. Among policy shapers in the federal executive branch, the newspaper lamented, *Losing Ground* had quickly become holy writ: "In agency after agency, officials cite the Murray book as a philosophical base" for proposals to slash social expenditures. A couple of months later, in *U.S. News & World Report*, contributing columnist David Gergen noted that Murray's book "forms the intellectual underpinnings for assaults upon social programs currently under way in Washington."

Media outlets marveled at the sudden importance of Charles Murray's work. *Losing Ground* "has been the subject of dozens of major editorials, columns, and reviews in publications such as the *New York Times*, *Newsweek*, the *Dallas Morning News*, and *The New Republic*—even the *Sunday Times* of London," wrote Chuck Lane in a March 1985 issue of *The New Republic*. The book's success "is a case study in how conservative intellectuals have come to dominate the policy debates of recent years." That domination, Lane concluded, was being enhanced by the think tank behind *Losing Ground*: "The Manhattan Institute's canny innovation is to rely as little as possible on chance—and as much as possible on marketing. Of course, money helps, too."

Nearly a decade later, *Losing Ground* was one of the central texts of the "welfare reform" debate. With the Wall Street Journal editorial pages showcasing anti-welfare commentary from Murray, the echo effects were swift and loud.

In mid-November 1993, George Will's syndicated column cited "what the social scientist Charles Murray calls an inner city culture of '*Lord of the Flies* writ large.' " Will concluded that the nation's "rising illegitimacy rate…may make America unrecognizable before political institutions recognize the necessity of measures as bold—as boldly traditional—as Murray recommends." The chorus of pundits expounding simultaneously on the same themes included Michael Barone, Joe Klein, Charles Krauthammer and John Leo.

At the same time, Murray was making the rounds of network TV shows, including ABC's *This Week*, where Will had previously lauded him. On Nov. 28, 1993, host David Brinkley introduced Murray with lavish praise as "the author of a much-admired, much-discussed book called *Losing Ground*, which is a study of our social problems." In minutes, Murray was explaining his solution: "I want to get rid of the whole welfare system, period, lock, stock and barrel—if you don't have any more welfare, you enlist a lot more people in the community to help take care of the children that are born. And the final thing that you can do, if all else fails, is orphanages."

Six months later, George Will was in typical form on *This Week*, misidentifying political scientist Murray as a sociologist along the way: "Charles Murray, a sociologist here in town, says the government must actively try to regenerate the stigma that attaches to illegitimacy. One way of doing that might be to abolish welfare."

By this time, Murray hadn't been at the Manhattan Institute for several years. He moved on to the American Enterprise Institute in 1990, "when the [Manhattan] Institute refused to support his research on differences in intelligence between blacks and whites," Stefancic and Delgado report in *No Mercy*, "taking with him his annual $100,000 foundation grant from the Bradley Foundation for salary, overhead, and other expenses." But, as Stefancic and Delgado put it, the Manhattan Institute "appears to have forgiven him: Shortly after *The Bell Curve* was published [in late 1994], the Institute sponsored a luncheon to honor Murray and the book, in which he proposes a genetic explanation for the fifteen-point difference in IQ between blacks and whites that is the basis for his dismissing affirmative action policies as futile."

Over the past ten years, the Manhattan Institute has raised a great deal of money from right-wing sources for designated book projects, with the Bradley Foundation alone contributing more than $1 million. Abigail Thernstrom has been one of the grateful beneficiaries. "The Thernstroms wrote their book with a $100,000 advance paid by the Institute," the *Philadelphia Inquirer* reported in October 1997. "Similar fellowships are given to other authors who espouse views that support the Institute's agenda." The resulting book co-written with Stephan Thernstrom, *America in Black and White: One Nation, Indivisible*, has borne gratifying media fruit for its backers.

Describing *America in Black and White* as "a benchmark new work" that "turns the accepted history of racial progress in America upside down," *Time* devoted three pages to the book in early September 1997. "Some of its points are compelling," the magazine concluded, although "the Thernstroms often construct tenuous arguments."

Some reviewers gave the book a chilly reception. In the *Los Angeles Times*, history professor Martin Duberman commented that it "provides an encyclopedic rationale for being all at once optimistic and inactive about racial divisions." But even when spiced with criticisms, the coverage frequently had the flavor of the review in *The New Republic*, which claimed that the Thernstroms' "tough-minded book serves the cause of racial justice." The big media response to the book, while mixed, had the effect of propelling the Thernstroms to center stage as credible researchers weighing in against affirmative action.

Along with ongoing subsidies from a number of large conservative foundations, the Manhattan Institute has gained funding from such corporate sources as the Chase Manhattan Bank, Citicorp, Time Warner, Procter & Gamble and State Farm Insurance, as well as the Lilly Endowment and philanthropic arms of American Express, Bristol-Myers Squibb, CIGNA and Merrill Lynch. Boosted by major firms, the Manhattan Institute budget reached $5 million a year by the early 1990s.

Dubbing it an "iconoclastic research group," a 1993 *New York Times* news article declared: "What distinguishes the Manhattan Institute is its work to translate its ideology into concrete proposals that appeal to a wide spectrum of political beliefs." The impacts have been national: "Despite its focus on New York, the Manhattan Institute has had its greatest influence in other cities. Mayors in Philadelphia, Indianapolis, Jersey City and Phoenix have praised it and adopted some of its advice." By 1995, the *Boston Globe* was calling it "one of the nation's most effective policy think tanks."

Many newspaper editors have been extremely receptive. "For its size," Stefancic and Delgado observe, "the Manhattan Institute publishes more op-ed pieces, including many on affirmative action, than any other think tank."

March 1998

Part XVII
Promoting Serious Absurdity

A Pop Quiz About News Judgment

With summer 1997 almost gone and schools back in session around the country, now is a good time for a pop quiz on news coverage.

Don't worry—this "test" won't be graded. It's up to you to decide which answers ring true.

Today's quiz is multiple choice.

1. When America Online gained control of CompuServe the other day, there wasn't much concern expressed in news media because:

   a) "Antitrust" is an obsolete idea that just belongs in history books.

   b) America Online was already huge, with 9 million subscribers, so 2.6 million more are no big deal.

   c) Key media conglomerates—like Disney, Westinghouse and Time Warner—have grown even larger because of recent mergers and buyouts, so they're hardly inclined to make an issue of such consolidation of media power.

2. Cyberspace continued to be a great subject for thousands of adulatory news stories over the summer because:

   a) Everybody loves to sit in front of computer screens.

   b) Color graphics are more nifty than ever on the World Wide Web.

   c) Few journalists seem bothered by the fact that the Internet is well on its way to becoming a medium that's mainly dominated by a few corporations.

3. Secretary of State Madeleine K. Albright recently visited a Jerusalem hospital for a widely reported photo-op with Israeli victims of terrorism. What are the chances that Albright will ever visit a Lebanese hospital for a photo-op with civilian victims of the periodic bombing raids by Israeli air force jets?

   a) Fifty-fifty.

   b) One out of 100.

   c) Roughly equivalent to the odds that you'll win a lottery and collect several million dollars.

4. The death of Princess Diana was the biggest American media story of the season. That's because:

   a) No other event in the world was more important.

   b) She was extraordinarily nice and helped a lot of charities.

   c) She was a glamorous mega-celebrity with stylish clothes who boosted TV ratings and magazine sales as soon as she died.

5. In their first two issues of September, the nation's top news magazines, *Time* and *Newsweek*, devoted all four covers and a total of 129 pages to Princess Diana's life and death. Meanwhile, those magazines ignored many issues that deeply concern a broad range of Americans. This is an example of journalism:

   a) Giving people what they want.

   b) Telling people what they want.

   c) Telling people what they want and then giving it to them.

6. Many American reporters and pundits explained that Diana was heroic because she struggled to overcome adversity as

a single mother. However, the same reporters and pundits are much more likely to vilify than praise this country's millions of low-income single mothers. That's because:

a) Princess Diana endured more adversity than impoverished single mothers do.

b) Princess Diana tried harder to be a good mom than they do.

c) Generally, news reporting and punditry are respectful of the rich and disdainful of the poor.

7. In the mainstream media, hundreds of stories and commentaries have been very critical of the paparazzi because:

a) Unlike the photographers who make big money by hunting down celebrities as quarry, the owners of mainstream media are committed to placing public service above profits.

b) It's moral to sell millions of dollars worth of TV commercials for repetitive specials about a dead princess but immoral to sell photographs of a live princess.

c) This has been a wonderful opportunity for mass-media outlets to tout their own moral superiority in a profitable manner.

September 10, 1997

Announcing
the P.U.-litzer Prizes for 1997

The P.U.-litzer Prizes recognize some of America's smelliest media achievements. Although journalists do not covet these annual awards, the competition remains fierce.

Each year, I sift through hundreds of entries with my colleague Jeff Cohen, who heads the media watch group FAIR. In 1997, many news professionals were deserving, but only an elite few walked off with a P.U.-litzer:

VULGAR EXCESS PRIZE—Columnist Frank J. Prial

In his "Wine Talk" column published by the *New York Times*, Prial declared: "The $100-a-bottle wine, once an example of vulgar excess, is now an everyday occurrence." Everyday occurrence for whom? Three days later, a chart in the *Times* business section showed that only 3 percent of California wines retail for over $14 per bottle; 59 percent sell for under $3.

RIGHT-WING DIVERSITY AWARD—Public Broadcasting Service

This fall, PBS moved to diversify public TV's schedule, which already includes a half-dozen weekly political shows hosted by conservatives like William F. Buckley, John McLaughlin, Ben Wattenberg and James Glassman. So a new PBS series, *National Desk*, features rotating hosts: White conservatives Fred Barnes and Morton Kondracke are joined by *black* conservative Larry Elder. Now that's diversity.

PUBLIC-GOES-PRIVATE AWARD—Bill Baker, president of PBS affiliate WNET TV in New York

Speaking to a corporate luncheon for representatives of ad agencies, Baker extolled the trends at the Public Broadcasting Service: "Welcome to the new PBS. Corporate messages on PBS get more creative every year. You can show products. You can use slogans." Maybe PBS now stands for the Privatized Broadcasting Service.

TABLOID TYRANT PRIZE—Publishing magnate Mort Zuckerman

During the height of Dianamania in September [1997], Zuckerman exercised his prerogative as owner of New York's *Daily News* by firing the top editor, Pete Hamill. The problem? Hamill tried to cut back on celebrity and gossip coverage. His last battle with management was over the use of a crude, revealing photo of Princess Diana exiting a car. Hamill lost the fight and the job.

ULTIMATE HEADLINE—New York *Daily News*

"Princess Di Knew O.J. Would Walk"

SATANIC AMERICA PRIZE—Rev. Sun Myung Moon and the *Washington Times*

Rev. Moon is the founder and funder of the *Washington Times*, the daily newspaper preaching conservative-style American patriotism. But Rev. Moon, leader of the Unification Church, has developed enormous contempt for the United States. In a May 1 speech, according to the *Washington Post*, Rev. Moon said: "The country that represents Satan's harvest is America." In another recent speech, he proclaimed that women in the United States are worse than prostitutes, that "God hates the American atmosphere" and that "Satan created this kind of Hell on the Earth." (None of these comments were reported in the *Washington Times*.)

OFF THE CHARTS AWARD—The *New York Times*

Last September, an elaborate chart in the *New York Times* appeared under a somber headline: "Making War on Israelis: A Deadly Rhythm Since Arab Autonomy." The chart was filled with a list of fatal attacks on Israeli civilians during the previous three years. Omitted was any mention of the killings of 144

Palestinian civilians by Israeli police and soldiers in the same time period.

"SERVICES NO LONGER NEEDED" PRIZE—Ambrose Evans-Pritchard

From 1993 through early 1997, British correspondent Evans-Pritchard was known as one of the wildest Clinton-bashing journalists in Washington. His reporting for the London *Sunday Telegraph*—widely circulated in the United States via the Internet and conservative talk radio—sought to link Bill Clinton to every imaginable conspiracy, from Arkansas drug dealing to Vincent Foster's "mysterious death." When Evans-Pritchard headed home to England in spring 1997, he gave this reason for leaving Washington: "Bill Clinton has become such a right-wing president that my services are no longer needed."

"YOU CAN'T SAY THAT ON TV" AWARD—CBS, NBC and ABC Networks

Thanks to thousands of ads urging consumers to buy this or that, TV networks are hugely profitable. But even a single ad urging people *not* to buy is apparently one too many. That's what anti-consumerism activist Kalle Lasn learned when he offered $15,000 for a network ad promoting "Buy Nothing Day," a 24-hour shopping moratorium on the day after Thanksgiving. The ad points out that "the average North American consumes thirty times more than a person from India." NBC rejected the ad, saying it doesn't "take any advertising that's inimical to our legitimate business interests." CBS's rejection letter said that Buy Nothing Day is "in opposition to the current economic policy in the United States."

Well, the sixth annual P.U.-litzer Prizes are now history. But more competition will soon be underway. And contestants begin 1998 with a clean slate.

December 17, 1997

And Now,
the P.U.-litzer Prizes for 1998

For the seventh year in a row, I have worked with Jeff Cohen of the media watch group FAIR to sift through the many entries for a P.U.-litzer Prize—the annual award that pays tribute to this nation's smelliest media offerings.

The competition to win a P.U.-litzer was never more fierce. Now, after long and careful deliberations, we are ready to reveal the P.U.-litzer Prizes for 1998.

LEWINSKY OBSESSION AWARD—Too Many Winners to Name

SILLIEST POLL QUESTION—Fox News Channel and MSNBC (Tie)

In January, Fox News asked the public to rule on Monica Lewinsky: "average girl" or a "young tramp looking for thrills"? After seven months of focusing on little else besides Clinton's (sexual) morals, MSNBC announced a poll question in August. "Clinton's morals: Should it be a political issue, or should it remain a private concern?"

SPONSORSHIP SMOG AWARD—*Time* magazine

Despite the fact that cars are the planet's leading source of smog, *Time* allowed the Ford Motor Company to be the exclusive sponsor of its environmental series "Heroes for the Planet." A *Time* editor admitted the arrangement was "fairly unusual."

WHO'S CALLING THE TUNE AWARD—Coca-Cola

A letter from Coke's ad agency to magazines demanded that Coke ads not appear next to articles on the following "inappropriate" topics: "hard news; sex-related issues; drugs (prescription or illegal); medicine (chronic illnesses such as cancer, diabetes, AIDS); health (mental or physical medical conditions); negative diet information (bulimia, anorexia, quick weight loss); food; political issues; environmental issues; articles containing vulgar language; religion." In other words, magazines should be as empty of nutrients as Coke is.

CORPORATE PARANOIA PRIZE—CNBC

Charles Grodin's nightly talk show on CNBC was known mainly for fixations on O.J. Simpson and Monica Lewinsky. Once every blue moon, however, Grodin veered from CNBC-preferred subjects to issues of consumer rights and the impact of draconian drug laws on poor people. These occasional, off-key topics were apparently too much for network bosses. In June, when CNBC cancelled the show, *Variety* reported: "One insider says the network finally got fed up with Grodin's nightly denunciations of the capitalist system." Grodin later returned to TV, confined to weekends on MSNBC.

THE JINGO-JOURNALISM AWARD—Charles Krauthammer

Frustrated with a lack of bloodshed after confrontations between the United States and Iraq, columnist Krauthammer waxed apoplectic in a Nov. 30 *Time* magazine article. He derided U.N. Secretary-General Kofi Annan as "the head of a toothless bureaucracy that commands no army, wields no power and begs for revenue." What's worse, Annan's diplomacy stalled the U.S. war machine. "It is perfectly fine for an American president to mouth the usual pieties about international consensus and some such," Krauthammer wrote. "But when he starts believing them, he turns the Oval Office over to Kofi Annan and friends."

TENDERNESS FOR TYRANTS AWARD—The *New York Times*

Continuing the tradition of empathy for the brutal Indonesian dictator Suharto that it had maintained for a third of a century, the *New York Times* repeatedly put the best face on the tyrant as pro-democracy forces challenged his grip on power last spring. According to the *Times*, Suharto was a "profoundly spiritual man" and a "reforming autocrat." The *Times* offered this rationale for the mass murderer: "It was not simply personal ambition that led Mr. Suharto to clamp down so hard for so long; it was a fear, shared by many in this country of 210 million people, of chaos."

LEFT OF FAR-RIGHT AWARD—Al Hunt of the *Wall Street Journal*

Hunt, usually about as leftward as anyone gets on CNN's *Capital Gang*, enthusiastically endorsed the renaming of Washington's National Airport after Ronald Reagan. In a Jan. 15 *Wall Street Journal* column, Hunt praised Reagan for busting the air-traffic controllers' union: "In the first month of the Reagan presidency, the controllers illegally went on strike…. The president alone hung tough, contending simply that an illegal action couldn't be countenanced. This was a man very comfortable and secure with himself, which arguably is the single most relevant consideration in choosing a president."

KILLING-HER-SOFTLY PRIZE—*Time* magazine

In its June 29 cover story—"Is Feminism Dead?"—*Time* bemoaned the alleged fading of authentic feminism. Meanwhile, *Time*'s top editors were pushing its strongest feminist writer out the door. After years as a regular columnist for *Time*, Barbara Ehrenreich found that her eloquent talents were no longer wanted there.

FEMINISTS-AS-PROSTITUTES-AND-NAZIS AWARD—Michael Barone of *Reader's Digest* and Larry King of CNN

On CNBC's *Hardball* program in August, former Congresswoman Elizabeth Holtzman noted that Monica Lewinsky appeared to be a consenting adult. An irate Barone exclaimed: "Basically, we've established the feminist movement in the United States, we've now found what profession they're in and the only question is their price." A few weeks later, on *Larry King Live*, feminist leader Patricia Ireland said that she disapproved of Clinton's conduct with Lewinsky but didn't think it warranted impeachment. King responded: "If you were a high-way-builder in Germany in 1936, you would have said, 'Let's keep Hitler because he built highways.' You're a highway man."

ETHNIC STEREOTYPE AWARD—Rush Limbaugh

On March 2, Limbaugh advised Madonna how to have a second child: "Well, Madonna, if this is what you want to do, just do what you did. Take a walk in the park. Stake out some gang-member type guy who looks like a hunk to you. Pay the guy some money. Bring him into the apartment on Central Park West, bed him and it can happen all over again just like it did the first time." The father of Madonna's first child, Carlos Leon, is a Latino. He has no known connection to any gang activity. When he met Madonna, Leon was a fitness trainer; Limbaugh's current wife had been an aerobics teacher.

FINGER ON THE (BLUEBLOOD) PULSE AWARD—*USA Today*

In a September story on consumer reactions to the stock market plunge, *USA Today* reported that "signs of some fallout have begun to appear." The signs? Reduced sales of Manhattan real estate, San Francisco yachts, Beverly Hills mansions and St. Louis Cadillacs, Mercedes, BMWs and Porsches. There was no mention of any impact on Americans who don't drive their Mercedes to the yacht club.

December 16, 1998

Index

292

Acknowledgments

Hundreds of people went out of their way to share ideas and information that ended up in this book. Thanks to all. In particular, I want to express appreciation to everyone at the media watch group FAIR. In the years since he co-wrote the "Media Beat" column, Jeff Cohen has always been generous with his astute suggestions. Jim Naureckas has been a fine editor of my articles for *EXTRA!* And Peter Hart has come through with many elusive facts.

For my weekly column, Julian Brookes often provided valuable research. And heartfelt thanks are also due everybody at Common Courage Press, especially Greg Bates, Rachel Coen and Arthur Stamoulis.

On the Institute for Public Accuracy staff, my colleagues Marguerite Hiken, Sam Husseini and David Zupan are a pleasure to work with. They do a lot to make the struggle worthwhile.

My parents, Miriam Solomon and Morris Solomon, have continued to encourage me with their wisdom.

Cheryl Higgins frequently improves my writing with her cogent insights. And she also helps me far beyond words.

About the Author

Norman Solomon writes a nationally syndicated column, "Media Beat," distributed to daily newspapers by Creators Syndicate and to weeklies by AlterNet. His commentary articles on media have appeared in the *New York Times, Washington Post, Miami Herald, Newsday, Baltimore Sun, USA Today, Los Angeles Times, Boston Globe,* Minneapolis *Star Tribune,* Atlanta *Constitution,* Cleveland *Plain Dealer, Arizona Republic, International Herald Tribune* and many other newspapers. Solomon has also written for periodicals such as *The Progressive, EXTRA!, In These Times, Z Magazine,* the *San Francisco Bay Guardian,* the *National Catholic Reporter,* the *Texas Observer* and *The Nation.*

His nine books include a series of three volumes co-written with Jeff Cohen—*Wizards of Media Oz, Through the Media Looking Glass* and *Adventures in Medialand.* In addition, Solomon co-authored (with Martin A. Lee) *Unreliable Sources: A Guide to Detecting Bias in News Media.* Solomon's other books published during the 1990s include *The Trouble With Dilbert: How Corporate Culture Gets the Last Laugh, False Hope: The Politics of Illusion in the Clinton Era* and *The Power of Babble: The Politician's Dictionary of Buzzwords and Doubletalk for Every Occasion.*

Solomon has appeared live on C-SPAN, CNN's *Crossfire,* NPR's *Talk of the Nation,* MSNBC, Fox News Channel and hundreds of radio shows around the United States. He is the senior adviser of the international radio program *Making Contact.* And he is a longtime associate of the media watch organization FAIR (Fairness & Accuracy In Reporting), which has a website at <www.fair.org>.

Norman Solomon is currently executive director of the Institute for Public Accuracy, a nationwide consortium of policy researchers. The Institute is on the Web at <www.accuracy.org>. Solomon lives in northern California with his wife, Cheryl Higgins. He can be reached c/o the publisher or via e-mail at <mediabeat@igc.org>.